Brazil and the Quiet Intervention, 1964

Texas Pan American Series

Brazil and the Quiet Intervention, 1964

by Phyllis R. Parker

University of Texas Press, Austin and London

The Texas Pan American Series is published
with the assistance of a revolving publication
fund established by the Pan America Sulphur
Company

Library of Congress Cataloging in
Publication Data
Parker, Phyllis R   1947–
    Brazil and the quiet intervention, 1964.

    (Texas Pan American series)
    Bibliography: p.
    Includes index.
    1. Brazil—Politics and government—1954–
2. Brazil—Foreign relations—United States.
3. United States—Foreign relations—Brazil.
I. Title.
F2538.2.P28   320.9'81'06   78-25856
ISBN 0-292-78507-0

To the memory of my father,
Mark H. Richards,
who was fascinated by foreign
countries and who respected
the well-written account.
I am grateful for that legacy.

CONTENTS

TABLES

PREFACE

There are values expressed at the formation of the United States and upheld in the greater moments of its history that affirm the necessary respect for the worth and dignity of man as a means of regulating society. These values include ideas of justice, equality, and freedom of choice, each defended as an inviolable human right. The men who created the United States assumed that the protection of these values was a reasonable and effective way of defining a nation's functions. There is, however, something disconcerting about dealing with U.S. foreign policy and these espoused values at the same time. U.S. policies seem structured to benefit the United States politically, economically, and militarily with little apparent regard for the impact these efforts have on the integrity of other nations' institutions. In this setting, the rights claimed in the Declaration of Independence sound increasingly like principles that apply only to the United States and its citizens often at the expense of those very rights for other peoples.

In Brazil in the early sixties, the erratic policies of the government of President João Goulart exacerbated the political unrest and economic troubles of the country. The U.S. response amplified Brazil's difficulties by lending support to national elements opposing the Goulart administration. U.S. actions ranged from political and economic sanctions and manipulations to military support for ridding Brazil of its president. That coup effected the replacement of Brazil's incomplete democracy with authoritarian military rule. Ambassador Lincoln Gordon and other U.S. officials suggested that Goulart's ouster had saved democracy in Brazil by confronting growing subversive elements in the government and society and by preventing Goulart's executing his own coup from the left in order to gain dictatorial powers.[1]

I believe that decisions by U.S. law and policy makers that affirm the value of the individual and respect his integrity are in the best interest of the United States and that if the United States is to have allies that respect both themselves and the United States it must approach these nations with a firm regard for the integrity of their institutions as well as for these principles. In my judgement, U.S. policy toward Brazil in the early sixties failed to take these values into sufficient account and thus contributed to yet another failure of institutions designed to safeguard individual freedoms and rights. My purpose in writing this book, however, is of narrower scope. It is simply to relate the story of U.S. activities in Brazil in the early sixties and what some of the more important actors said at the time and later remembered about these events.

This study draws heavily upon documents declassified in the Lyndon Baines Johnson[2] and John F. Kennedy presidential libraries. I should note, however, that only the declassified portions of those documents that made their way to the White House files have been examined and not all of the communication between the U.S. embassy diplomats and their Washington counterparts. Some of the more sensitive portions of those documents of which the White House did receive a copy remain classified and inaccessible. Equally important, the archival materials I investigated are communications between U.S. policy makers about their perceptions of events. This singular perspective has been reinforced by interviews and letters with some of those individuals involved in formulating and implementing U.S. policy during the 1964 crisis. I have had no opportunity to examine Brazilian primary sources,[3] and this deficiency is only partly remedied by the use of secondary studies. Corroboration of some of my findings has come from the incredibly generous offer of John W. F. Dulles to make available the notes from his many interviews with a number of Brazilians who were involved in the planning or the execution of the 1964 coup. These notes, which at the time were unpublished, enabled me to refine interpretations that would otherwise have been based on U.S. sources alone.

There are many others I would like to thank for their contributions to this work. I am grateful to the staff at the State Department for giving me access to files from the early sixties. I especially wish to thank Robert Ballantyne, who headed the Brazil Desk at the department, for his interest in my research.

I am grateful to Capt. Thomas V. Solan (U.S. Navy) and to Col. James Record (U.S. Air Force) for their assistance in reading military cables. In addition, Colonel Record was most helpful during all of my research as a liaison with Pentagon sources. I also wish to thank Debi Tucker for her assistance in locating research materials in the Washington, D.C., area.

I want to thank the staff at the Lyndon Baines Johnson Presidential Library in Austin, Texas, and particularly archivist Martin Elzy for his assistance in locating and declassifying documents. I also wish to thank the staff at the John F. Kennedy Presidential Library in Waltham, Massachusetts, especially archivist Megan Desnoyers for help in my use of documents there. There were other libraries that were valuable resources in the researching and writing of this book: The Lyndon B. Johnson School of Public Affairs Library and the Nettie Lee Benson Latin American Collection, both at the University of Texas at Austin, and the Library of Congress in Washington, D.C. I am grateful to the staff at each of these libraries for their assistance.

This book grew out of an independent research project at the Lyndon B. Johnson School of Public Affairs. I wish to thank Henry David and Sidney Weintraub, members of the faculty, who were my advisors in the project. I appreciate their guidance and their ready encouragement and support.

In addition to archival materials and federal agency and congressional sources, this book draws heavily upon interviews with some important American figures who helped to shape this story. I am grateful to Vernon Walters, former defense attaché, for his valuable time and for the interesting stories he remembers from the period and to Thomas Mann, former assistant secretary of state for Latin American affairs for his time and interest in sharing his memory of events as well as his thoughts on the political theories behind the events. I am particularly indebted to former Ambassador Lincoln Gordon for his frank and detailed responses. In the interviews and in subsequent contacts, Dr. Gordon has been unfailingly generous toward me. I should note that, while these interviews provide important links in understanding the progression of events, the opinions and conclusions drawn from them and from the other research materials are mine and these gentlemen may disagree with my interpretations. It is a truism that hindsight should provide added clarity that might not have been available in the daily rush of living events. If this book is diminished because of any disagreements I might have with a policy judgement, the fault, once again, is mine and not theirs.

For reasons I regret, I am not at liberty to thank publicly one person whose help was substantial and valuable to me both personally and professionally. I am grateful nonetheless.

Finally, I wish to thank my family who have, in numerous ways, helped me in my research and writing. My special thanks goes to my husband, David Parker, who typed the manuscript and who has been a constant source of constructive criticism, support, and inspiration.

Brazil and the Quiet Intervention, 1964

INTRODUCTION

In 1958 Brazil's president, Juscelino Kubitschek, proposed "Operation Pan-America." He envisioned a dramatic economic development program to attack the critical problems of human misery that fomented political unrest in Latin America. The Eisenhower administration showed only slight interest.

In January 1959, Fidel Castro overthrew the Fulgencio Batista regime, and over the next two years the Cuban revolutionary government established strong ties with the Soviet Union. Alarmed at the potential spread of communism in the Americas, the United States became more responsive to an assistance program of positive action in Latin America.

On March 13, 1961, President John F. Kennedy proposed a new approach for U.S. assistance to Latin America: the Alliance for Progress. This program was to be a multilateral mobilization of the American nations' efforts and resources against the vast social and economic inequities that beset them. For the United States it meant the re-orientation of its fragmented Latin American aid programs into a program of regional scope generously funded for democratic development.

The charter for the Alliance for Progress was signed at Punta del Este, Uruguay, in August 1961 by all the members of the Organization of American States (OAS) except Cuba. The charter established grand goals for the next decade: economic growth and diversification, a more equitable distribution of income, elimination of adult illiteracy by 1970, access to six years of primary education for all children, improved public health conditions, increased low-cost housing, and a strengthening of regional economic integration with the vision of a Latin American common market.[4]

As part of the plan, the signatories agreed to adhere to democratic principles and to establish national social and economic development programs based on the concept of self-help. They also agreed that the developing countries would be assisted with outside capital of at least $20 billion of mostly public money over a ten-year period and that the least-developed countries would be given priority in this assistance. The charter established guidelines for long-term economic development, for immediate and short-term action measures, and for external assistance from the United States in support of national development programs. Finally, it set up an organizational structure, including an expert review procedure for the national plans that all participating countries were to prepare.[5]

Success in Brazil, the largest and most populous nation in Latin America, was important to the success of the new program. Brazil was a constitutional democracy and a nation of spectacular potential, with abundant resources, developing industrial centers, and a growing middle class; but Brazil was also plagued by social and economic problems—staggering poverty, a largely disenfranchised agricultural sector, a chronic balance of payments problem, and a high rate of inflation. Brazil was fertile ground for the message of hope, whether from the left or from such programs as the Alliance for Progress. In Brazil, however, U.S. policy makers would be increasingly frustrated by fiscal inconsistencies in that government's policies and by a president who seemed to encourage a redistribution of power and structural changes within that system that, it was believed, might result in a communist or socialist-oriented country less tied to the United States.

This book proposes to trace U.S. policy toward Brazil through the turbulent Goulart administration. I treat the role of the United States in Goulart's overthrow in some detail, in order to provide a context for the considerations by U.S. policy makers that led the United States to support a coup in 1964 and to back generously the succeeding military dictatorships.

A Gaucho Becomes President

On August 25, 1961, Jânio Quadros unexpectedly resigned as president of Brazil after less than seven months in office. His vice-president, João Goulart, was out of the country at the time on a good will tour of eastern nations, including Communist China, Poland, and the U.S.S.R.

Vice-President João Belchior Marques Goulart, a wealthy land owner, cattle breeder, and lawyer from the state of Rio Grande do Sul, was 43 when Quadros resigned. "Jango," as he was popularly known, had built a political base in labor as a protégé and controversial labor minister of Getulio Vargas (president of Brazil from 1934 to 1945 and 1950 to 1954). As minister, Goulart was active in reforming labor legislation, but he was accused of collaborating with communists, radical militants, and labor leaders.[6] The military caused his ouster from the cabinet after Goulart attempted to alter the relation between the minimum wages of civilian laborers and army enlisted men in favor of the former.[7]

Although a member of the upper class, Goulart was a populist, in that he sought his support from the people rather than through the more traditional party structures. His lack of personal exposure to the problems of the working class, however, caused some to believe that

Goulart simply exploited the growing labor sector for personal political gain.[8] He remained in national politics after leaving Vargas' administration and was elected vice-president under Juscelino Kubitschek in 1955 and again under Quadros in 1960. Former U.S. Ambassador Lincoln Gordon has suggested that Jango's gaucho background may explain a certain pride he took in physical strength and in displays of power and thus in his political style.[9] He lacked talent, and some say interest, in managing the daily activities of government.[10]

The resignation of Jânio Quadros brought on a crisis over legal succession to the presidency. The three military ministers in the cabinet, General Odílio Denys, Brigadier Gabriel Grün Moss, and Admiral Silvio Heck vigorously moved to block Goulart's return to Brazil as president. The Congress proposed an alternative to the exclusion of Goulart: the creation of a parliamentary system. Determined to prevent Goulart's assumption of the presidency, the military ministers began organizing the armed forces and put controls on the media.[11] They issued a manifesto accusing Goulart of having dealt with "agents of international communism," and charging that he might promote infiltration of the Brazilian armed forces, turning them into "simple Communist militias."[12] The effectiveness of the military was weakened by a split between those who favored Goulart's leftist leanings and those who desired to see the constitution legally upheld. To block Goulart's assumption of power was clearly illegal and, as it turned out, impossible without the full support of the armed forces.[13]

A compromise was finally reached, and on September 2 the Congress passed an amendment called the Additional Act that established a modified parliamentary system. On September 7, 1961, João Goulart was sworn in as president of the United States of Brazil under this parliamentary system.

Two New Ambassadors

During this two-week presidential succession crisis in Brazil, Lincoln Gordon appeared before the U.S. Senate Foreign Relations Committee for confirmation as ambassador to Brazil. Gordon, a summa cum laude graduate of Harvard, had been a Rhodes Scholar at Oxford, where he had earned a Ph.D. in economics. He had an impressive background both in and out of government. He had been a professor of government and administration at the Harvard School of Business and, as consultant to the State Department, had been a member of a task force that had helped create the Alliance for Progress.[14]

Gordon postponed assuming his new post until after the Brazilians had settled the presidential issue. On September 14, one week after Goulart became president, the State Department sent a briefing memorandum to President Kennedy describing what the U.S. position toward the new government in Brazil would be: "Pending the clarification of U.S. orientation, we propose to deal with the new government on the assumption that there has been no break in the continuity of the traditionally close and cordial relations between the United States and Brazil. As for President Goulart, we are prepared to give him the reasonable benefit of the doubt, while trying to encourage him to believe cooperation with the United States is to his and Brazil's advantage."[15] The concern of the Brazilian military ministers over Goulart's past political associations was shared by U.S. policy makers. That they specified a willingness to grant him a "reasonable benefit of the doubt" seems to suggest that from the beginning, Goulart's motives were regarded with some suspicion. The briefing memorandum went on to say that the United States would honor previous commitments, but that any new assistance would be "based on an understanding that the government of Brazil would pursue its economic program under conditions of financial stabilization and would support and carry out the objectives of the Alliance for Progress."[16]

Ambassador Gordon arrived in Brazil on October 3, 1961. His first request of Niles Bond, who had been chargé d'affaires in the interim, was that he explain the division of power between the president and the prime minister. Bond replied that no one really knew, but that it was reported that Jango had recently said that he "had no intention of being reduced to a 'Queen Elizabeth,'" meaning he did not accept the notion of his presidential powers having been removed or limited by the Additional Act.[17]

Ambassador Gordon soon presented his credentials to Goulart and became personally acquainted with the president. His principal contacts in the government, however, were San Tiago Dantas, foreign minister, and Walter Moreira Salles, finance minister, and, to a much lesser extent, the prime minister, Tancredo Neves. Gordon's first months were busy as he set about establishing the Alliance for Progress in Brazil. He and his staff worked with Goulart and his cabinet on matters of shared interest —debt rescheduling, aid programs, and Goulart's proposed visit to the United States.[18]

Just before he resigned the presidency, Quadros had appointed Roberto de Oliveira Campos, a career diplomat and one of Brazil's leading economists, as ambassador to the United States. With Quadros' resignation, Campos had given up the idea of going to Washington, but his friends Dantas and Neves encouraged Goulart to retain him. Goulart did call Campos, and he told him that even though he differed with Campos politically and he considered Campos too conservative he wanted Campos' services in Washington. Campos asked the president for instructions, but Goulart replied that he had not had time to think closely about foreign policy and referred Campos to Dantas for instructions.[19]

Campos arrived in Washington and presented his credentials to President John F. Kennedy in October of 1961. Kennedy questioned the new ambassador about the parliamentary system, wondering if it were viable and whether or not it would open the way for leftist infiltration and radical movements in the country. Campos related his beliefs that parliamentary systems work best when few parties are in the system (Brazil had twelve parties at the time) and that much depended on the vigor and effectiveness of the new cabinet.[20]

Two Omens for the Future

A Profits-Remittance Law—Differences between Friends

On November 29, 1961, the Chamber of Deputies passed a remittance of profits bill that raised the question among the U.S. business community in Brazil of whether Brazil, which had traditionally welcomed foreign private investors, was becoming a hostile business environment. The U.S. business sector in Brazil argued that the $30 to $40 million being remitted to all (not just U.S.) foreign investors annually did not deserve the accusations that the investors were "suction pumps" and that they were "bleeding . . . the Brazilian economy."[21] The bill had a number of provisions that would inhibit foreign investment: Reinvested profits would be considered national capital and, therefore, not a part of the base for computing remittances.[22] Annual remittances of profits out of Brazil would be limited to 10 percent of registered capital, with no provision covering the depreciation in the value of the Brazilian currency. Moreover, existing Brazilian businesses could not be bought out by foreign firms; foreign companies would not be able to borrow from Brazilian banks; and all Brazilian residents would be required to declare their holdings.[23] That bill did not become law, but the concept of limiting profit remittances became a topic of debate in both houses. The prospect of the passage of such measures dampened foreign investment in Brazil and was a point of deep concern to U.S. business interests and, hence, to U.S. diplomats.

Military Solutions: Plans for a Golpe

It was in late 1961 or early 1962 that Ambassador Gordon met Admiral Heck, one of the three military ministers under Quadros who had opposed Goulart's return to Brazil as president. The meeting was arranged, at the admiral's request, by his niece who had known Gordon since 1946 when he had been a delegate and she an interpreter to a United Nations convention on atomic energy.[24]

After an informal supper party, Admiral Heck and the ambassador talked. The conversation was in Portuguese, which Gordon understood but could not yet speak with facility. The admiral told Gordon that Goulart was a "dreadful character" and "communist" and that he was "up to no good," and he warned that Goulart was only "pretending to act good now." Heck informed the new ambassador that large numbers of civilians and military were organizing a *golpe* against Goulart, proudly attributing the greatest percentage of conspirators to the navy. Heck told Gordon that he was not requesting American help but that he had wanted the ambassador to be informed. He added, "One of these days we will act, and I hope when that happens, the United States will not be unsympathetic."[25]

Gordon was surprised at what he heard. He managed a few words of appreciation to the admiral for sharing this story and assured Heck he would keep the conversation in mind. This approach was the first of many to Gordon and his staff.

When Gordon returned to the embassy, he cabled the State Department and informed his top staff about Admiral Heck's story. The ambassador requested that the embassy CIA (Central Intelligence Agency) section expand their traditional intelligence gathering concerning the far left to find out what was going on in the country from all perspectives, and he asked specifically if they could check the validity of Admiral Heck's story. In addition, Gordon asked the three U.S. military attachés if they had any information about a conspiracy against President Goulart.

The reports that came back to the ambassador suggested that Admiral Heck's story was not true. U.S. intelligence sources indicated that while Goulart had been friendly with communists, the allegation that he was a communist and the story concerning a concerted effort to remove Goulart appeared to be false. The reports did say that, quite apart from his politics, there were some who believed Goulart to be incompetent, a conclusion which Gordon himself eventually reached. Meanwhile, the ambassador laid aside stories of conspiracy and turned to more pressing matters.[26]

Brazil's Independent Foreign Policy

Following the pattern that Quadros had established, the Goulart administration attempted to pursue an "independent foreign policy," which had been widely publicized and had gained some national popularity. This policy de-emphasized entangling alliances and included friendly overtures to Communist bloc nations as potential friends and trading partners with Brazil.[27]

Ambassador Gordon realized that this line of policy under Goulart, as under Quadros, was in practice substantially friendlier to the United States than to the Communist bloc.[28] Some U.S. policy makers, however, were alarmed by a lack of tractability in Brazil's policies. In a position paper regarding Brazil's independent policy, written for Secretary of State Dean Rusk before an OAS meeting at Punta del Este in January 1962, Deputy Assistant Secretary Richard Goodwin wrote: "the political situation in Brazil is extremely precarious. We have no choice but to work to strengthen this government since there appears no viable alternative."[29]

The United States had hoped that the OAS would adopt mandatory sanctions against Cuba at that January meeting.[30] Deputy Goodwin and Ambassador Gordon, however, urged Secretary Rusk to take a more moderate line. Gordon suggested that Rusk instead seek to secure "effective moral isolation without mandatory sanctions." His purpose was to avoid the possibility that the OAS might adopt a position in which Brazil would vote with the minority and in which the majority votes would represent the small, less-populated countries of Latin America. The ambassador feared that "this would place very heavy strain on an already weak government situation, and would probably stimulate a leftist campaign for the denunciation of the whole inter-American treaty structure."

Gordon believed that if the measure passed with Brazil in the dissenting minority, the Brazilian government "would be confronted with a dramatic and clear-cut conflict between their treaty obligations under the Rio Pact and the notion of an 'independent' foreign policy . . . a major theme of the new government."[31]

Gordon's advice showed an understanding on his part of the political situation in Brazil, as well as an awareness of the potential implications in Brazil of an exacting position by the United States. At the meeting, Brazil's Foreign Minister San Tiago Dantas and U.S. Secretary Dean Rusk argued the point of mandatory sanctions, and Dantas was openly critical of Rusk for the United States' anti-Castro position. Following Brazil's independent policy line, Dantas would not agree to expel Cuba from the OAS or to impose economic or diplomatic sanctions as such against Cuba.[32]

Communist Cuba was a raw nerve for U.S. policy makers and Dantas could not convince Rusk to accept a position of "coexisting recognition" that would impose a statute of limitation with negative obligations for Cuba involving "refusal to enter into an armed pact with the Soviet group, discontinuation of the practice of demoralizations of governments in Latin America, subversive activities, and propaganda, etc."[33] Several years later, when Roberto Campos reflected on the conflict between the United States and Brazil at that Punta del Este meeting, he said, "I found that Saxons are not as rational as they claim to be. In this particular instance of Cuba, they were extremely emotional and quite irrational."[34]

The Domestic Scene

A Poor Economic Inheritance

Goulart inherited an economy weakened in part by the very rapid growth ("Fifty-Years' Progress in Five") policies of the former president, Kubitschek. A U.S. embassy analysis of the Brazilian economy as of January 1961 stated, "The Bank of Brazil has practically no foreign exchange reserves and the Kubitschek Government has exhausted virtually every recourse 'ethical' and 'unethical' available to it for the purpose of covering the balance of payment deficit . . . so as to permit President Kubitschek to leave office on January 31 under apparently solvent circumstances."[35]

Quadros entered the presidency endorsing a balanced budget and a favorable climate for foreign investors. His anti-inflation program earned him the initial approval of international lending institutions and in May and June, he announced successful negotiations with foreign creditors.[36] Quadros began to alter his austerity program. By August when he resigned, his monetary authorities were already exceeding the domestic money-supply limitations required by his foreign creditors.[37] The stabilization effort begun by Quadros had completely collapsed by the end of 1961. A State Department study in March 1962 of Brazil's financial situation noted that inflation in Rio during the last quarter of 1961 had increased more than 50 percent on an annual rate.[38]

In December 1961 the United States released $40 million of a $338 million loan negotiated in May of that year, bringing the total amount released to Brazil to $209 million. The Brazilians were informed at that time that the remainder would be forthcoming only after the United States "was convinced that Brazil was carrying out a

sound stabilization program." Ambassador Gordon amplified the U.S. position, discussing with Brazilian financial
officials areas of concern to the United States, including
Brazil's support of an unrealistic exchange rate (a policy
which tended to strengthen import demand and discourage exports), excessive bank credits for the private
sector, wage increases to government workers, and the
need for taxes on other revenues to cover costs. Finance
Minister Salles developed new stabilization plans that
were approved by the cabinet on March 15, 1962.[39] Pending U.S. assistance and the forthcoming presidential visit
by Goulart to the United States at Kennedy's invitation
appear to have influenced the content and timing of these
plans.

Communist Affiliations

Economics was never Goulart's forte and, like most poli-
ticians, he found the austerity measures requisite to stabilization plans to be unpalatable. The president walked
a tightrope, trying to appeal to foreign groups for financial
support and to consolidate domestic support with the
hopes of regaining full presidential powers. To reassure
the more conservative element of Brazilian society, Goulart expounded on his anticommunist sentiments and his
belief in the democratic process.

To some observers, however, his actions and affiliations
indicated otherwise. John W. F. Dulles in his book *Unrest
in Brazil* details some of Goulart's activities with labor
and peasant organizations that alarmed anticommunist
elements in Brazil.[40] U.S. labor organizations and U.S.
embassy officials noted with concern that Brazil's labor
leadership was "increasingly receptive to communism."[41]

In March 1962, just before Goulart's visit to the United
States, a CIA memorandum sent to the White House reported that Raul Francisco Ryff, Goulart's press secre-

tary, had been a member of the Brazilian Communist
Party (PCB) since 1932. The report said that Ryff's appointment immediately after Goulart was inaugurated
had concerned some Brazilians who believed Goulart
might follow "an openly Communist course," and that the
president had "resisted pressure to remove Ryff from his
immediate entourage."[42]

Expropriation: A Domestic-Foreign Conflict

Consolidating domestic and foreign support was made
more difficult for Goulart by his brother-in-law, Leonel
Brizola, governor of Rio Grande do Sul. Brizola, who was
extremely nationalistic in his politics, was a vocal and
emotional advocate for thoroughgoing structural changes
in Brazil. On February 16, Brizola disrupted preparations
for Goulart's visit to the United States by expropriating
an International Telephone and Telegraph (ITT) subsidi-
ary located in his state.[43] The next day, Harold S. Geneen,
president of ITT, sent President Kennedy an "urgent"
and "confidential" telegram alluding to a Cuban re-
semblance in "the irresponsible seizure of our American-
owned properties" and urging Kennedy to "take an immediate personal interest in the situation."[44]

Officials in both governments were concerned that the
ITT matter be settled before the Goulart visit to the
United States in April. Brazilian officials involved in the
negotiations included Foreign Minister Dantas, Ambassador Campos, and Rio Grande do Sul Secretary of In-
terior and Justice Brochada da Rocha.[45] Ambassador
Gordon was instructed by the State Department that
while he could not be an "advocate" concerning specific
proposals for settlement, he was nevertheless to "give
fullest possible support to [the ITT] efforts [to] obtain
prompt and adequate compensation, utilizing in this regard [the] full weight and influence [of the] U.S. Government."[46]

Fearful that the ITT case would not be immediately settled, officials at the State Department devised other strategies for countering the bad press that Brazil was receiving in the United States and communicated their suggestions to Ambassador Gordon. They emphasized that an announced change in the profits-remittance bill would improve the climate. Gordon was also told that "if you are able to report that negotiations with [the] government of Rio Grande do Sul under [the] aegis of GOB [Government of Brazil] are moving ahead favorably, President Kennedy will make optimistic answer to planted question at press conference on March 7."[47]

The State Department also indicated that an announcement by Brazil of a firm commitment to a stabilization program would help and could be a basis for approving additional drawings under the 1961 Quadros aid package.[48] Loan approval based on Finance Minister Salles' stabilization program was completed after Goulart arrived in Washington, and Brazil was authorized to draw $35 million immediately with the balance of the agreement to be paid May 31, pending the effective execution of Salles' program.[49]

The ITT negotiations continued beyond Goulart's visit in April, and in direct response to the extended negotiations in Brazil the U.S. Congress passed the Hickenlooper Amendment as a rider to the 1962 Foreign Aid Bill.[50] This amendment obligated the U.S. government to suspend assistance to any country that had expropriated U.S.-owned property unless that country demonstrated that it had taken steps to make speedy compensation for the full property value within six months.[51]

The Presidents Meet

In July 1961 President Quadros had been invited to visit the United States as a guest of President Kennedy in December of that year. The visit had been canceled after Quadros' resignation. Goulart's invitation to come to Washington was, to some extent, an outgrowth of the earlier invitation to his predecessor. An early visit to the United States was important to Goulart in building his domestic and foreign prestige; the visit could promote the stability of his new government by adding respectability to his administration and by mollifying the military and the conservative elements, which viewed as suspect Goulart's past left-wing associations.[52]

Officials at the U.S. State Department considered Goulart to be "not an ideological leftist" but rather a "thoroughgoing opportunist," who "upon taking office assumed the mantle of a political moderate seeking constructive reform in his country." It was the State Department position that

> whatever the motive for Goulart's obvious desire to be invited here, he is the President of the most important nation in Latin America—a nation comprising one-third of the region's population and land area, in which are centered all the economic, social and strategic problems to which the Alliance for Progress is a response. . . . Given the significance of our success in Brazil for the entire Alliance for Progress program, it is in our interest to try to persuade Goulart that cooperation with us is in his and Brazil's best interest. In any case, it is in our interest that, as chief executive of a potential world power, he clearly understand the directions of our policy in Latin America and elsewhere and what we hope to accomplish.[53]

Because of Goulart's special ties to labor, Ambassador
Gordon suggested that the AFL-CIO play an active part
in the Goulart visit and that U.S. labor leaders take advantage of the "opportunity to express forthrightly to
President [Goulart] their concern over communist attempts to gain control of labor movements in Latin America's largest and most important country."[54]

President Kennedy greeted Goulart personally when he
arrived at Andrews Air Force Base on Tuesday morning,
April 3. Later that day, Kennedy was host at a White
House luncheon in Goulart's honor. It was a colorful gathering with guests from a variety of backgrounds.[55]

That afternoon Goulart and Kennedy, accompanied by
staff and diplomats from both countries, met to discuss
substantive issues. The expropriation of the ITT subsidi-
ary had not been settled, and Kennedy emphasized the
need for procedures for prompt, adequate, and effective
compensation for nationalized properties. Goulart ad-
hered to the notion of peaceful nationalization through
negotiated settlement but requested that payments be
stretched over a long period in order to ease the financial
strain on the reconstituted companies and to minimize the
foreign exchange burden for Brazil. The two presidents
left the matter in basic accord.[56] It was to become a
source of irritation to the Americans that this agreement
between presidents did not expedite expropriation settlement procedures.

Kennedy followed up on Gordon's previously expressed
concern with "Communist attempts to gain control of
[the] labor movement" in Brazil.[57] Goulart appeared to be
irked at the great emphasis that the United States gave
to what he considered to be a highly exaggerated problem
and told Kennedy that, although communists might have
an exaggerated share in labor leadership, he felt confident
that he could handle any problems that might erupt. Kennedy, perceiving Goulart's touchiness on the subject,
hastened to interject that his had only been meant as a

friendly comment and that he did not wish to intervene at all in Brazilian affairs.[58]

Goulart and Kennedy also discussed some of Brazil's economic problems. Goulart complained of the restrictive attitude being taken by the Export-Import Bank. Kennedy offered to contact officials at the bank personally; however, Ambassador Campos never detected any additional cooperativeness by the bank to indicate that Kennedy had indeed spoken with them.[59]

Goulart was host at a reception at the Brazilian embassy to which members of the Washington diplomatic corps and business and government officials were invited. President Kennedy attended the luncheon briefly. After this large affair, there was a small private dinner upstairs at the embassy, attended by the Brazilian group and several "Kennedy men," including Walt Rostow, Arthur Schlesinger, Richard Goodwin, John Kenneth Galbraith, Lincoln Gordon, Ted Sorensen, and Robert McNamara. The purpose of the dinner was to have a frank discussion on pertinent issues of shared interest.[60]

McNamara, commenting on Brazil's strategic importance, indicated some apprehension about the "leftist infiltration" in Brazil and asked for some clarification of Brazil's neutral stand in foreign policy. Ambassador Campos suggested that "neutralism" was an inadequate term and explained that "what was involved was really a deep urge of the Brazilian people to assert their personality in world affairs."[61]

Ambassador Campos later related Goulart's pleasure over a discussion the Brazilian president had had at the dinner with Galbraith concerning inflation. Galbraith criticized orthodox financial policies and Brazil's acceptance of International Monetary Fund (IMF) domination and suggested that the orthodox Indian economists might benefit from the buoyancy created by Brazil's inflation. Goulart was delighted to discover this liberal attitude on the part of at least one of Kennedy's advisors. Campos countered Galbraith by suggesting that Brazil was "risking having inflammation rather than inflation." Galbraith's wit and charm as well as his accommodating posture struck a responsive chord with the Brazilian president. Ambassador Gordon was annoyed at this turn of the conversation.[62]

During this trip, Kennedy and Goulart talked both in meetings attended by diplomats and privately about the question of military coups. Goulart was suspicious of alleged U.S. interference in the deposing of Frondizi in Argentina and warned Kennedy of the danger of encouraging military coups. Kennedy assured Goulart that there had been no U.S. participation in the Argentinean event and that the United States opposed military coups, but Goulart remained unconvinced. Ambassador Campos said later: "I don't believe that Goulart ever really believed him and subsequently in several of my conversations with Goulart he always brought up the point of American intervention and American sympathies for military regimes. I tried to dissuade him from this viewpoint but it was sort of a basic fundamental suspicion which he never really abandoned."[63]

Ambassador Gordon had the impression that Goulart believed that the Americans had never caught up with Russia since the Sputnik space shot, so the ambassador arranged a trip to the Strategic Air Command (SAC) Base at Omaha, Nebraska, before Goulart returned to Brazil. General Amauri Kruel, friend and advisor to Goulart and head of the Casa Militar, accompanied the Brazilian presidential party on this trip. Gordon was pleased that Kruel seemed particularly impressed by what he saw in Nebraska. As the Brazilians were leaving the SAC base, Kruel requested that Gordon convey his thanks to General Thomas S. Power (SAC commander) and added, "You can be certain I will tell my colleagues that the future of the 'free world' is in good hands."[64]

Return to Brazil

Goulart returned to Brazil with his image much improved in both the United States and Brazil. According to Ambassador Campos, Goulart had dreaded a possibly hostile reception in Washington and was pleased with the cordial tone of the visit. Goulart had been impressed by Kennedy —his personality, his liberal posture, and his advisors— and it appeared that Goulart might become a Latin American supporter of the Alliance for Progress.[65]

The bond Goulart felt between himself and Kennedy began to weaken as he returned to the daily administrative activities of his office. The ties with Washington could not eradicate the many economic and political problems that faced the Brazilian president—problems for which at times there appeared to be no answers or for which all solutions portended negative consequences. The excitement of Washington dimmed as domestic issues jostled for attention: the financial crisis, his own lack of power, and the growing demands from the left. The parliamentary system was a thorn that began to irritate. More and more Goulart focused his energies on proving the unworkability of that system and on gaining full presidential powers.

On May 1, Goulart made a speech demanding "basic reforms" for Brazil and calling for a constitutional amendment to change the requirement that landowners whose land is expropriated must be paid in cash.[66] Ambassador Gordon interpreted the speech as Goulart's "new tack to the left."[67]

According to a CIA report, Goulart told Finance Minister Moreira Salles in mid-May that he had definitely decided to resign.[68] Goulart had had a mild heart attack in Mexico on his return trip from Washington. He had refused to take the two or three weeks of full rest urged by his doctors and remained sensitive to discussions about his health.[69] He may have considered resignation because of his health. Another possible motive is that Goulart was vacillating after his recent speech and felt unsure of his position. Whatever the reason, by the end of May, Goulart had reconsidered and decided against resignation, at least for the time being.

Gordon presented Goulart with a large color photograph of the Andrews Field welcoming ceremony when they met on Saturday, May 26. The president seemed genuinely pleased. The ambassador used the visit to follow up on a number of items discussed in Washington.[70]

Gordon urged Goulart to take stronger fiscal control measures. The ambassador said that for the first time he saw a "real danger of runaway inflation in Brazil unless counteraction [were] taken." The ambassador criticized payrolls padded for political appointment purposes; and, although Goulart agreed that the practice was a "sham," Gordon knew that as president, Goulart had countersigned such nominations.[71]

Goulart indicated that he would support collaboration with the United States on oil shale production. Because the Soviets had made efforts to penetrate Brazil's petroleum industry and because of the technical knowledge to be gained, the U.S. Defense Department shared with the Brazilian military a strong interest in the strategic significance of Brazilian oil shale development. It was hoped that the venture might also alleviate the major drain on Brazil's foreign exchange caused by petroleum imports— over $200 million annually.[72]

Leonel Brizola had made a strongly anti-U.S. speech earlier that week and Gordon suggested to Goulart that he believed it would be helpful if Goulart "could make clear his disagreement [with the] Brizola position." Goulart responded that his family relationship with Brizola "in no way signified similar political views," but he would not promise the ambassador any public disavowal of his brother-in-law.[73]

At the meeting, the ambassador thought that Goulart was preoccupied with the limitations placed on him by the parliamentary system, and, in fact, Goulart complained of the lack of action from the Congress or his ministers. Goulart told Gordon that he believed the cabinet and the Congress had lost so much prestige that if he wished, he "could arouse people overnight to demand [the] shutting down of Congress," but he added that he did "not want to take such an anti-constitutional line."[74]

The Parliamentary Crisis

Under the parliamentary system, all cabinet members were to be members of Congress; and, since the constitution stipulated that no one could run for Congress who had held an executive position during the previous ninety days, Prime Minister Tancredo Neves and his entire cabinet resigned June 26, 1962, in order to establish their eligibility to run for office in October of that year.[75] From the perspective of U.S. State Department officials, Goulart "seized the opportunity to create an artificial crisis to further his desire to regain the full powers of the Presidency."[76]

Goulart submitted to Congress a nomination for San Tiago Dantas to replace Neves. Dantas had recently made a speech urging policies backed by popular interests, such as agrarian reform. The Congress tended to represent vested interests, and Dantas' nomination was not confirmed.[77]

Gordon was pleased with Goulart's choice of a replacement for the Dantas nomination, Auro de Moura Andrade,
whom the ambassador described as "center or right of
center."[78] Within forty-eight hours of his becoming prime
minister, however, Moura Andrade resigned. As it turned
out, Goulart had secured an undated resignation from
Moura Andrade before his appointment. He used the
document after arguing with Moura Andrade over names
for cabinet posts and after the new prime minister indicated that he would not work for an early plebiscite on
the parliamentary system.[79]

Goulart next nominated Francisco Brochado da Rocha
who had been a legal advisor to Brizola in the ITT case.
Gordon viewed Brochado da Rocha as politically far left,
temperamental, excitable, a "mystic," and "not entirely
sane." Congressmen, eager to return home to begin cam-
paigning for the October elections and also wanting to
avoid being blamed for prolonging the crisis, approved the
nomination.[80]

President Kennedy had planned to visit Brazil that
July, but Gordon suggested that the visit be postponed
until the government was more settled. Both presidents
agreed and the trip was deferred until the following
November.[81]

Meanwhile, Brochado da Rocha, in an emotional appeal,
submitted a program to the Congress calling for large
transfers of power to the cabinet. The program failed to
pass the Congress and on September 13, Brochado da
Rocha and his cabinet resigned. Three days later Congress set the date for a plebiscite on the presidential
question: January 6, 1963.[82]

October Elections

The October 1962 elections in Brazil were of keen interest to the United States. They presented the United States with a chance of exerting some influence at the state level in favor of measures similar to those it was promoting without great success at a federal level. President Kennedy, in February 1962, sent a message to Fowler Hamilton, administrator of the Agency for International Development (AID), saying: "I feel that we should do something of a favorable nature for Brazil before the election this Fall, which is going to be crucial. Perhaps a food, water or some other project could be proposed. Would you talk to Ted Moscoso about this and then discuss it with me."[83]

Riordan Roett, in *The Politics of Foreign Aid*, describes how, in Brazil's northeast, U.S. monies were allocated to projects that would benefit conservative gubernatorial candidates with the hopes of influencing those elections in favor of anticommunists.

In one of the more important races the tactic was unsuccessful. Miguel Arraes whom the State Department described as "the commie-lining Mayor of Recife," won the election for governor of his state, Pernambuco. Roett's allegation that U.S. economic assistance tried to influence that electorate was substantiated by a State Department official who said U.S. distrust of Arraes and concern for the political drift in Pernambuco had prompted the United States, against the advice of some State Department officers, to give heavy funding to the Companhia Pernambuco de Borracha Sintetica (COPERBO), a plant designed to use sugar in the production of synthetic rubber. Cid Sampaio, who had backed Arraes' conservative opponent, had interests in COPERBO.[84]

Gordon later admitted that the planning and approval process of COPERBO was not sufficiently careful because of the politics involved.[85]

Nor was this, Gordon has since acknowledged, the only case of U.S. intervention, citing specifically the U.S. monies that went directly to support the campaign of certain candidates in the 1962 elections. The ambassador later recalled: "Undoubtedly it was much more than a million dollars, and I would not be surprised if it had gone as high as five million dollars. But it was not an enormous sum, it was not dozens of millions of dollars. There was a ceiling per candidate. . . . Basically, the money was to buy radio time, to print signs, that type of thing. And you can be sure that many more requests were received than were honored."[86]

Goulart Salutes the Yankee Victory

A New Defense Attaché

About one week after the Brazilian elections, a new defense attaché arrived at the U.S. embassy in Rio de Janeiro. Colonel Vernon Walters was a brilliant linguist. He had served as interpreter for the World War II Brazilian Expeditionary Force that had fought in Italy with the Allied Forces under General Mark Clark. This shared experience was the background for the strong friendly ties between Walters and a number of leaders in the Brazilian military.

Walters had met Lincoln Gordon when the two men had worked together on the Marshall Plan in the late forties.

The ambassador had made a special request to have
Walters transferred to Brazil. When Walters reported to
Gordon and asked for instructions, the ambassador replied, "I want to know what's going on; I want to be able
to influence activities in the country. And," he added,
"I don't want any surprises." Later, Walters was to
reminisce: "He was never surprised." As defense attaché,
Walters gathered military intelligence. Walters' many
wartime friendships were to be very helpful sources
to him as he sought information about the Brazilian
military.[87]

Missiles in Cuba

All U.S. ambassadors to Latin America were contacted
on October 21, 1962, and informed that the United States
had discovered Soviet missile installations on Cuba. The
ambassadors were instructed to seek out the heads of
state in their countries two to five hours before 7:00 P.M.
Eastern Standard Time—which was when President Kennedy was scheduled to announce this discovery to the
nation and to the world on television and radio and to
inform them of the impending message. An official com-
muniqué would be sent for the heads of state.[88]

Gordon took his new defense attaché with him to meet
Goulart and to add a "show of uniform." Kennedy's message arrived late and the last section was hand-delivered
by an embassy messenger to the palace soon after Gordon
and Walters arrived. Walters read aloud, translating the
English message into Portuguese. Goulart listened with
rapt attention, following the English script over Walters'
shoulder. When Walters came to the section of the com-
muniqué that stated that "missiles have arrived or are on
their way," Goulart indicated that he had been following
events in the press and had been left with the impression

that "Rusk said only a couple of weeks ago that those were only defensive weapons."[89]

Gordon was impressed with Goulart's apparent acceptance of the gravity of the situation. When Walters completed the translation, Goulart took a deep breath and said: "if what Kennedy says is true, then this is not just a threat to you but to all of us—and, of course, we are with you." Goulart seemed almost disappointed that the United States was stopping short of direct military action. He asked why the United States did not "just blow them all up with an atomic bomb?" When the ambassador reminded him that such an action would kill thousands of people, Goulart retorted, "Well, what do you care? They're not Americans." Goulart was eager to keep abreast of the situation. He told Gordon he would not be leaving town and that he wanted to see the ambassador each day for a briefing.[90]

Kennedy's handling of the Cuban missile crisis served to raise his stature in the eyes of Goulart, and public opinion in general in Brazil was quite favorable to the turn of events.[91] On Saturday, when it was clear that the Russians had backed down, Gordon went again to give Goulart his daily briefing. Goulart greeted the ambassador and said, "Let's go upstairs and have a drink." Ambassador Gordon did not generally drink anything alcoholic but agreed. Goulart poured two generous measures and seemed to wait for a toast from his guest. Gordon said some words about world peace and prosperity to which Goulart responded with a grin and a wink: "Hell no! To the Yankee victory!"[92]

A Special Emissary from the President

President Kennedy's trip to Brazil, postponed in July and rescheduled for November, was postponed once again after the Cuban missile crisis. The idea developed during November staff sessions at the U.S. embassy in Rio, that Goulart might be influenced to "confront the communist problem" as well as to deal seriously with Brazil's economic difficulties if President Kennedy's brother Robert could visit Brazil that year.[93] The embassy staff hoped that Goulart might use his influence to counter the growing numbers of organizations, particularly among labor and student groups, which U.S. officials considered to be inspired by communist leaders and basically unfriendly to the United States.

A meeting to discuss the possibility of a trip by Robert Kennedy was held at the White House, attended by Ambassador Gordon, President Kennedy, Attorney General Robert Kennedy, Secretary of State Dean Rusk, CIA Director John McCone, and officials from the State Department. The trip was envisioned as an effort to enlist Goulart's support to counter Brazil's disturbing "drift to the left."[94]

In contrast to the presidential visit in April, Robert Kennedy's seems poorly conceived or at least haphazardly executed. Ambassador Campos was miffed at not being included in the planning of the trip. He recalls being informed at an embassy luncheon, "practically on the eve of Kennedy's departure." Campos advised officials at the State Department against the proposed trip, which he thought was poorly timed. The reaction he received was that the United States hoped to influence the composition of Goulart's future cabinet in order to assure continuing cooperation between the two countries. Campos responded: "Well, in the first place, it's quite inappropriate to try to influence the composition of the Cabinet, and secondly, I don't think that Goulart will say anything relevant to you right now. You ought to wait for him to win the plebiscite and then if his government choices are such that a working arrangement would be difficult to establish, then bring the case to him."[95] Campos believed that a visit by Robert Kennedy at that time and for that purpose would complicate matters. The visit might be construed as an ultimatum that could embitter Goulart and might be followed with other negative reactions by the Brazilian president in order to maintain his public image of independence.[96]

The December 17 meeting of Robert Kennedy and Goulart in Brasilia was a disappointment for U.S. officials. Goulart believed that Kennedy vastly overrated communist infiltration in his government and suggested that Kennedy be more specific in his accusations. Gordon, who was present at the meeting, gave as examples the unions of Petrobrás, the federal oil monopoly, and of the postal and telegraph agency and offered to back up Kennedy's concerns with specific names. Goulart, while not denying that some workers in those agencies might have communist leanings, stated that he was in full control of the situation. Goulart seized the opportunity of the meeting to discuss other problems in United States–Brazil relations from his perspective, such as declining prices in Brazilian exports compared to rising costs for equipment that Brazil imported from the United States.[97]

Robert Kennedy's visit appears to have been taken as an informal ultimatum that did not really describe what the alternatives to Alliance for Progress programs and cooperation would be. Goulart later related to Ambassador Campos that it was as if he had been told that he had no capacity for judging the men surrounding him.[98] Both countries anticipated the plebiscite with some hope. With full presidential powers restored, Goulart could give full attention to being, instead of becoming, president.

Presidential Powers Restored

On January 6, 1963, the plebiscite was held. The purpose on which Goulart had increasingly focused his energies during the past year and a half was finally realized. Full presidential powers were restored to him by a margin of six to one. For the next five months, Goulart turned his attention to dealing with the economic and political problems that he had inherited and that his policies of the past months had amplified to critical proportions. Inflation in 1962 had been 52 percent. Cabinet ministers had come and gone with frequency over the past month. The machinery of the government had continued to operate, but without any consistent direction to give it stability or purpose.

With his full powers restored, Goulart appointed a new cabinet. San Tiago Dantas assumed the important position of finance minister. Dantas had served as foreign minister in Goulart's first cabinet and his candidacy for prime minister had been rejected by Congress the previous summer because they considered him too much a hero of the left. In spite of this past negative reaction to Dantas, he appeared to be a good choice, for he was respected by both liberals and conservatives nationally and internationally.

Working with Dantas and also in a cabinet level position (economic planning, without portfolio) was Celso Furtado, well-known past director of the Superintendency for the Development of the Northeast (SUDENE), the development agency for Brazil's Northeast, the country's largest backward area. Furtado had received his doctorate in economics at the University of Paris. President Kennedy had met Furtado in July of 1961 and had been impressed by his work in the Brazilian Northeast.[99]

Intellectually, Dantas and Furtado appeared to be good choices for designing and administering Goulart's economic stabilization and development programs. Politically they were identified with the left, but a more moderate left than Brizola's radical position.[100] It seemed plausible that unpopular measures of austerity might be more palatable to the left opposition when proposed by these men and within the context of a larger package of planned reforms.

Neither Dantas nor Furtado, however, had a strong political base. For their program to succeed, Goulart needed to use his office to muster the domestic support necessary for success of the program. In addition, it would be important for domestic political consumption that any international negotiating done by Dantas and Furtado be acceptable on Brazilian terms; if it were to appear that they gave too much for too little, any political support they had might dissipate in the political rhetoric of the radical left.

Furtado directed the preparation of the Plano Trienial do Desenvolvimento Economico e Social, 1963–1965 (Three Year Plan for Economic and Social Development) during the last three months of 1962.[101] The plan became the basis for the Dantas program.

Critics assailed the lengthy plan as a compilation of statistics and trends designed not to depict reality, but to create an optimistic projection.[102] The purpose of the plan was to control inflation and maintain growth while eliminating bottlenecks within the system by introducing fiscal and agrarian reform measures. The plan projected the maintenance of a high level of public investment as an essential element to continued economic growth, which would be financed by new taxes on the wealthier sectors and by reducing government subsidies of industries. Critical to the financing of this comprehensive package was a refinancing of Brazil's foreign debt.[103] While the plan also required a more aggressive export program that would assure foreign exchange for imports necessary for continued industrialization, it also depended on Brazil's receiving $1.5 billion in foreign government aid and $300 million in foreign private investment during the three years.[104]

Ambassador Gordon's response to the plan was that in spite of technical deficiencies, "the broad purposes of it were, we thought, good . . . [it had] all the essential elements of a combined stabilization and development program." Gordon approved Dantas' energetic attack on inflation through removal of import subsidies, credit limitations, limiting wage increases, and certain budget economy measures.[105]

Early in 1963, after Goulart had announced his new cabinet, Ambassador Gordon and Ambassador Campos were invited to Brasilia to dine with the president at the Alvorada Palace. During the dinner Goulart turned to Ambassador Gordon and said, "You've seen my list. I remember our conversation with Robert Kennedy. What do you think?" Lincoln Gordon considered the cabinet a "mixed bag" as far as "communist influence" was concerned and told Goulart quite frankly that he was quite concerned about the labor minister, Almino Afonso, whom the embassy judged to be "very red" and a threat because he "allowed communist infiltration in unions." Goulart responded that he was surprised Gordon had not favorably mentioned Dantas who would be handling his economic program.[106]

Economic Stabilization for Assistance:
The Bell-Dantas Agreement

The U.S. Climate

A Gallup poll in early February of 1963 was brought to the attention of President Kennedy. A survey indicated that public opinion was "that the U.S. should be a little more discriminating in its dispersal of foreign aid funds, [and that] of particular irritation to some Americans [were] cases where countries receiving such aid have turned against [the United States] in international disputes."[107]

On March 4, David Bell, AID administrator at the State Department, briefed the president by memorandum on what he believed would be the major theme of the report soon to be released from the Committee to Strengthen the Security of the Free World, an executive committee chaired by General Lucius D. Clay. The Clay committee had studied U.S. economic and military aid programs. In relation to Latin America, Bell indicated that the committee opposed "'bail out' assistance except where accompanied by the performance (not just the promise) of improved budget and fiscal policies." Bell agreed with this position, adding that "we can and should require stronger self-help measures by Latin American countries—and the issue will confront us almost immediately in connection with . . . Brazil."[108] The Clay report would be read by the U.S. Congress, and the performance of U.S. assistance programs would be measured against its stipulations when the U.S. Congress made appropriations for 1964. It would strengthen the case of those requesting aid appropriations if they could show that foreign assistance was not money thrown away and could be tied to the performance of the recipient country.

Such was the mood at the State Department when

Foreign Minister Dantas arrived in Washington in early
March to negotiate with U.S. officials for the generous
financial assistance upon which the Three Year Plan had
been based.

Dantas would have preferred postponing his trip to the
United States until he had time for applying some measures for economic recovery and could approach the negotiations from a stronger position. He had no choice, however. Brazil's plight was indeed desperate; assistance had
to come quickly or Brazil might be forced to default on
some foreign debt payment.[109]

Holding the trumps of the aid giver as the two countries
approached the bargaining tables, the United States assumed a posture of "limited and continuous cooperation."
Dantas had made numerous calls to Ambassador Campos,
trying to get some advance indication of the magnitude
of assistance the United States would consider. U.S. officials, however, remained silent before the actual negotiations. Gordon, who had flown up early to help develop
the U.S. position, said later: "We didn't actually do any
negotiating until March . . . when Dantas came to Washington. We considered that this was part of the strategy;
this would hold out a carrot and help influence things in
the desired direction."[110]

Actually, in spite of reservations over Brazil's economic
and political performance over the previous year, which
had been disastrous from a Washington perspective, the
United States was disposed to work with Dantas. The
position established by Gordon and State Department officials "was that the Three Year Plan, Dantas as Finance
Minister, and the kinds of policies he was supporting were
the best bet in sight, that if the program were carried
through it had real chances of getting Brazil out of its
economic difficulties of the year before, and that it was a
good basis for collaboration."[111]

The United States wanted assurance that Goulart

backed Dantas in commitments his finance minister might make, so Dantas brought two letters signed by Goulart (drafted by Dantas) to President Kennedy.[112] One dealt with negotiations in process in Brazil for the nationalization of the American Foreign and Power Company (AMFORP) and stated that he looked forward to a settlement soon after the U.S. Congress met, which would be in a few days.[113]

The Case for Brazil

The second letter masterfully pleaded Brazil's case in the coming negotiations. Goulart cited the principles of the Alliance for Progress, in which each nation had the right to determine its own destiny and goals of development, and, referring to U.S. postwar assistance to Europe, suggested underdevelopment and instability could be dealt with more effectively if each country could rely on an "adequate level of external cooperation as has been the case with other nations in other regions." Goulart reminded Kennedy that "economic remedies must be adapted to the reality of the social environment in which they are to be used"; to do otherwise could actually weaken that nation's economy and could "result in social rebellion and . . . open the way to dangerous forms of unrest." He spoke of a solution to which his government was committed (the Three Year Plan) as the only option "capable of harmonizing economic stability, the preservation of social peace, and the continuity of democracy." Goulart assured Kennedy that should "this cooperation not be available, we will not thereby abandon our fidelity to democratic principles" and closed by alluding to the importance of Brazil and the potential repercussions the case might have on other nations.[114]

At the negotiations, Dantas and Campos argued that with the establishment of the stabilization program of the

Three Year Plan there would initially be unavoidable
negative internal repercussions, such as rising prices re-
sulting from subsidy eliminations. Dantas and Campos
tried to persuade the U.S. negotiators that "even though
the disbursements might be graduated and geared to performance . . . the commitments should be generous and
forthcoming." Campos reflected later: "We needed then
an external victory and demonstration of foreign confidence, of foreign support and assistance that would
strengthen politically the hand of those that were seeking
stabilization."[115]

The Agreement

While the U.S. negotiators (AID Administrator David
Bell, Ambassador Gordon, and State Department officials)
approved of Dantas' plans for stabilizing the Brazilian
economy, their wariness of Goulart's intentions made
them doubt Dantas' ability to carry out this program. The
United States agreed to provide immediate stopgap assistance to Brazil totaling $84 million and an additional
$314.5 million in assistance for fiscal year 1964, pending
Brazil's negotiating long-term financial assistance from
such other sources as the IMF, the World Bank, and
Western European countries and Japan.[116]

The $314.5 million was tied to performance measures
agreed to by both sides and outlined in a letter from
Dantas to Bell. Dantas cited such actions already taken
by the Brazilian government (most of which were included
in the Three Year Plan) as termination of certain subsidies, the issuance of a plan for containing budget ex-
penditures, and limits placed on credit and on public
employee wage increases. In addition, Dantas made commitments to negotiate for additional funding from the
IMF and from Japan and Europe, to direct Brazil's for-

eign economic policy toward reducing Brazil's balance of payment deficit, to expand exports, to encourage foreign private investments, and to increase taxes and improve tax collection.[117]

For Dantas, the restrictive agreement was a bitter pill to swallow. At first Campos advised him not to sign it, but after the two men discussed their options they decided that neither they nor Goulart had enough national backing to implement the austerity program that would be necessary if all foreign assistance were severed and that that kind of support would have required an extreme nationalist spirit in Brazil that could backfire out of their control. One possible repercussion of rejection would also have been a break in relations with the United States. With no good choices available (from his perspective), Dantas signed the agreement "with a very heavy hand" and returned to Brazil to try to pull together support sufficient to allow him to carry out his economic development program.[118]

From the U.S. perspective, considering events of the previous year, the Bell-Dantas Agreement was fair, generous, and good for both sides. The United States had maintained its position of linking assistance with performance. These negotiations could be an example to the U.S. Congress of foreign assistance tied to a purpose. The agreement also sent a clear message to Goulart—that the United States would not and could not unilaterally rescue Brazil and warned him that U.S. assistance could only be a part of a much larger program for economic development and stability. From the U.S. perspective, the agreement, although "tough," contained the essential components for pulling Brazil out of its economic quagmire. The United States recognized that the agreement was bitter medicine and tried to dilute the harsh effects of an austerity program with the initial $84 million forthcoming immediately. Gordon remarked later that he thought "what he [Dantas] got was a great deal."[119] The ball was now in Goulart's court and U.S. State Department and embassy officials were watching closely.

Conspiracy in Brazil

Goulart's actions were also being followed by conservative elements in the Brazilian military, which in turn were being studied by the CIA. A CIA "Current Intelligence Memorandum" dated March 8, 1963, described plotting against Goulart by conservative groups in the military, led by retired Marshal Odílio Denys, minister of war during the administration of Jânio Quadros. Denys had evidently indicated that a coup depended on Goulart's first making a move that would precipitate widespread support for a countermove, but the CIA was concerned that "a premature coup effort by the Brazilian military would be likely to bring a strong reaction from Goulart and the cashiering of those officers who are most friendly to the United States."[120]

Application of the Plan in Brazil

Dantas returned to Brazil to try to implement the Three Year Plan. The austerity measures were being felt in sensitive areas. With the wheat subsidy gone, bread prices rose; with the oil subsidy removed, transportation prices —including urban bus fares—rose. The cruzeiro was devalued to meet the IMF requirement for a unified exchange rate, causing a rise in import costs and thus in the cost of living.[121] Dantas had agreed to limit wage increases for public employees to 40 percent, effective in April.[122] By mid-May, the cabinet had capitulated to the ensuing anger of the military and the civil servants and had agreed to 70 percent increases.[123]

According to Campos, Goulart viewed the agreement as "proof of U.S. mistrust and that embittered him and further deviated him from the road of cooperation."[124] The president expressed his disappointment when he met with Ambassador Gordon in early April. Gordon suggested the agreement was a good basis for cooperation and reminded Goulart that the government of Brazil "was suffering from [a] history of broken promises" and that it would take "time and effort on both sides" to rebuild confidence.[125]

At that meeting, Gordon further commented on his concerns about Brazil and mentioned Brizola's "campaign of agitation," and Labor Minister Almino Afonso's "not cooperating on wage policy" and moving to legalize the "procommunist" General Workers Command (CGT). Gordon reminded Goulart that the settlement of the AMFORP case had again been postponed and suggested that the continued postponement "raised [a] question of [Goulart's] personal good faith." Goulart seemed offended by Gordon's use of the word "stealing" to describe how he believed the Brazilian Congress wished to settle the AMFORP case. Gordon suggested to the president that if Brazil defaulted on a $30 million payment, due in ten days, it would bring Brazil to the "brink of the abyss" with repercussions at the IMF and the U.S. Congress, as well as in Brazil itself which would be faced with shortages of foreign exchange to buy essential imports. Goulart wondered gloomily if the economy were not already in the abyss, to which Gordon responded with assurance that "sensible action" could solve the problems and that Brazil's "longer run economic prospects [were] very bright."[126]

At the meeting, Goulart complained of delays in U.S. responses to Brazil's request to purchase military airplanes; Brazil was considering purchasing the helicopters from Poland. Gordon indicated that while it was his decision, "he could not expect the U.S. to like it, since it would break [the] line on [the] military source problem."[127]

Gordon described the farewell between himself and Goulart after this meeting as "cordial"; however, it is apparent that the State Department was assuming an increasingly unyielding posture. This position, it was hoped, would result in Goulart's seriously attacking what State Department officials saw as the growth of left-wing and communist groups within Brazil and giving the full backing of his office to the economic development program outlined in the Three Year Plan and elaborated in the Bell-Dantas agreement. Goulart's response was far from U.S. desires.[128]

In late April, the Brazilian government appeared to reach an agreement to purchase AMFORP for $135 million, following the tentative arrangement made between Goulart and Kennedy the year before in Washington: 25 percent of the settlement was to be paid in dollars and 75 percent was to be reinvested in Brazilian nonutility holdings. The settlement was attacked for its generosity by both the right and the left in Brazil.[129] Goulart, finding this agreement unpopular—in the context of other domestic battling over economic issues—tried to disassociate himself from its origins.[130]

President Kennedy personally inquired about developments in Brazil. A State Department brief written in response was supportive of Dantas and acknowledged the tremendous odds he faced. A team from the IMF was to arrive in Brazil on May 10. Continuation of U.S. funding through the Bell-Dantas Agreement was predicated on Brazil's also obtaining funding through the IMF. The State Department, casting about for ways to lend Dantas some much-needed support, was toying with the idea of sending a letter to President Goulart from President Kennedy. The proposed letter "would express admiration and support for Goulart's stabilization and development program with appropriate complimentary reference to Minister Dantas."[131]

A New Cabinet: The Plan Falls Apart

The letter was never sent. In June, Goulart replaced his entire cabinet, sounding the death knell for the Bell-Dantas Agreement. Ambassador Gordon watched events in Brazil with dismay. In his eyes, the dismissal of the cabinet marked a significant turning point in Goulart's administration. He testified later before the U.S. Senate Foreign Relations Committee: "Then started the . . . phase from July until the ending of the regime in March 1964 in which it became increasingly evident that the President's purposes were, in fact, to overturn the regime himself in the interest of a personalistic dictatorship . . . modeled after Perón in Argentina or Vargas, his mentor."[132]

In fact, however, the new cabinet represented the center and not what Dantas would have called the "negative left." Dantas' replacement was the former governor of São Paulo, Carlos Alberto Carvalho Pinto.[133]

An Appeal to Kennedy

Goulart had an encounter with Kennedy in Rome on July 1, 1963, the day after Paul VI was elevated to the papacy. At that meeting, Goulart requested a ninety-day postponement of the AMFORP settlement, assistance in encouraging Germany to give Brazil some long-term financing based on expected iron-ore exports, and postponement of payment on a U.S. Treasury loan and an Export-Import Bank payment.[134]

The two presidents exchanged letters later that month. In the exchange, Kennedy suggested direct negotiating

with AMFORP; Goulart responded that negotiations
should not be isolated but should be a part of overall
collaboration between Brazil and the United States.[135]
Repayment of the Treasury loan was postponed ninety
days, but the United States opposed Brazil's proposal to
borrow money in Germany because earnings from iron-
ore exports were a major source for servicing the Brazilian foreign debt.[136]

Goulart Administration Drifts to the Left

Growth of Communism in Student Groups

Cables between the State Department and the U.S. embassy and consulates in Brazil suggest that U.S. influence
and the power of people and groups friendly to the United
States was eroding.[137] In July the National Students'
Union (UNE) met in a suburb of São Paulo, for its annual
congress. The U.S. consul general in São Paulo, Daniel
M. Braddock, sent a description to the State Department
of "communist"-oriented candidates having won a land-
slide victory over what he considered the "democratic
slate."[138]

Braddock suggested that "given the difficulty of over-
coming the incumbent machine, there are one or two possibilities for end-runs." He believed that while direct suf-
frage (as opposed to the delegate system) would be an
improvement there was no assurance that the students
would not vote as their delegates had. Braddock suggested a second possibility, "to found competing student
organizations outside the framework of the UNE. These
groups would not have Government sanction and could

not vote in elections, but at least they might furnish a base around which the anti-communist students could pull themselves together."[139]

Goulart and the Military

The single most powerful group in Brazil is and was the military. The constitution entrusted the military with the mission "to defend the country and guarantee the Constitutional powers and law and order."[140] Goulart understood the importance of military support within the Brazilian system and set out to obtain it by surrounding himself with military leaders whom he believed would be loyal to him.[141] U.S. Defense Attaché Vernon Walters perceived a disturbing pattern in Goulart's appointments. In August 1963 Walters sent the Pentagon a report in which he stated:

> Ultranationalist officers who support President Goulart get promoted and get troop commands and desirable locations. Outspokenly pro-democratic pro-U.S. officers don't generally get promoted. They get passed over and retired or go to directorates as well as less desirable assignments, and other positions which do not involve troop command. A few colorless neutrals get promoted so that it cannot be said that only ultra-nationalists get promoted, and a few—very few—pro-U.S. officers may get promoted or have their assignments improved. To the great mass of uncommitted officers who want to get ahead and want good assignments, it is clear that the only way to get both is to follow the ultra-nationalist line.[142]

In addition to promoting military leaders who appeared to be most loyal to him, Goulart tended to give support to noncommissioned officers when they came in conflict with higher military authorities. On September 12 military discipline was visibly threatened when a group of sergeants demonstrated in Brasilia for soldiers to be allowed to hold elective office. Goulart's neutral response angered the Congress, which had become acutely aware of its vulnerability when the noncommissioned officers succeeded in holding prisoner for a time the president of the Chamber of Deputies and a Supreme Court justice.[143]

Aid to Brazil: Criticism in Washington and Brazil

The U.S. Congress was battling with Kennedy over his foreign aid bill. The House recommended that Kennedy's request be cut drastically. The bill was before the Senate Foreign Relations Committee when General Lucius Clay collaborated with the White House to send letters to newspaper editors throughout the country in support of foreign aid as a component essential to U.S. security.[144]

David Bell made a television and radio broadcast with Senators Clark and Scott of Pennsylvania on September 22 in which Senator Scott questioned Bell about U.S. assistance to Brazil, calling it "a bottomless pit." Bell assured the senators that the State Department was holding Brazil to its commitment to carry out an anti-inflation program, and Bell explained that while some project assistance for poor areas was continuing, "the main things, the large amounts of money which we would be prepared to provide by way of investment, capital, additions to Brazil—these are being held up until the Brazilians undertake and carry through the steps they can and should do."[145] The U.S. policy was indeed to link aid to performance, but a public statement to that effect made the U.S. position that much firmer; this statement, in fact, represented a foreign policy trend.

Gordon and his staff reviewed the Bell-Dantas Agreement in late August and decided that conditions were not being met. Gordon no longer actively sought to implement that agreement. The policy changed toward emphasis on project loans, loans tied specifically to an activity, as opposed to program loans that provide general assistance to the whole development effort and are related to macroeconomic policy. This new policy came to be known at the embassy as support for "islands of administrative sanity." The United States would not continue to support the central government, but aid would be given in individual cases "when the recipient was performing according to Alliance for Progress standards."[146]

The hardening line from Washington toward Goulart's government and the policy of dealing increasingly with state and local governments and individual agencies in loan commitments and disbursements was criticized in Brazil. In early September (before Bell's television appearance), Governor Miguel Arraes leveled a verbal assault on the United States and Ambassador Gordon at a meeting of local officials in the Northeast where the ambassador was a guest of Celso Furtado. Arraes was bitter because the United States had supported, for political reasons, projects that aided his opponent in the governor's race in Pernambuco in 1962. He subsequently had had a committee study U.S. aid in Brazil and unexpectedly used the northeastern meeting as a forum to release the committee report. He attacked the Alliance for Progress and accused the United States of intervening at the expense of the federal Brazilian government, through its aid programs, in state and local politics.[147]

Gordon was able to blunt the immediate barbs of Arraes's attack by responding to the report at the meeting. He talked about the AID program and said that, while the United States did indeed deal with state and local governments, all loans required a release by the Brazilian government, so nothing was being done outside the purview of the central government.[148]

There were complaints by Brazilians that the Alliance for Progress AID program was bogging down. In January, a U.S. political officer from the São Paulo consulate met with Fernando Correa da Costa, governor of the state of Matto Grosso. The governor was discouraged about the slow response to a mid-1962 request for U.S. assistance in building a hydroelectric plant in his state. The embassy officials had been initially encouraging, and the Brazilians had completed a large, detailed study containing required information for the U.S. officials. In the following year and a half the governor had only received vague encouragement from the embassy and requests for new studies—one of which had been completed, another was in preparation. Governor Costa expressed doubt that the project loan would be completed before his term expired in January of 1966. As the officer was leaving, the governor said that he had been reading *The Ugly American*, and he had found striking similarities between the book and his experiences.[149]

Considering Militant Solutions

On October 4, at the urging of his military ministers who were concerned over the growing numbers of strikes and incidents of political violence, Goulart requested that martial law powers be granted him by the Congress.[150] Congress delayed action on this state of siege proposal, which came under attack from many sides. To the consternation of his advisors, Goulart followed the path of least resistance and withdrew the petition on October 7.

During the month of October Goulart escaped a poorly executed kidnapping attempt in which his archenemy Carlos Lacerda, governor of Guanabara, appears to have been peripherally involved. In response to this attempted kidnapping, plans were made, apparently at the presidential palace, to have paratroopers arrest Lacerda.

Some of the officers refused to take part in the plot and warned the governor. The would-be abductors arrived late because of car and traffic difficulties. Lacerda exploited the publicity with gusto in his Rio newspaper.[151]

Goulart was unpopular with the Congress. He was distrusted by the right for his friendships with the left, and his brother-in-law, Brizola, led the attack from the left because his programs were not radical enough to change the system.

Brizola turned to the mass media and toward the end of 1963 he could be seen and heard on his television and radio stations in Rio, flanked by uniformed marines, calling for the people to organize into vigilante "groups of eleven." Each group was instructed to arm itself and to prepare to support an uprising against opposition. Upon request, Brizola offered to send the group a copy of Ché Guevara's handbook and other guerrilla information. These organizations were extremely nationalistic in spirit; and, while their presence and purpose was disturbing, the threat they posed was probably overrated.[152]

Criticism of the United States

In mid-November 1963 the second annual meeting of the Inter-American Economic and Social Council was held in São Paulo. The purpose of the meeting was to discuss techniques for better coordination of the Alliance for Progress.[153] Goulart made a speech in which he pointedly avoided reference to the United States and only mentioned the Alliance for Progress once. The speech stressed Brazilian leadership in Latin America against North America and the idea of building a bloc of underdeveloped nations against the developed nations. Ambassador Gordon was angered by the speech.[154] Roberto Campos, who believed that there was substance in the concept of international trade being promoted by Goulart, had argued against this planned emotional appeal at the council meeting. It was for him another disagreement with the Goulart administration that he was representing.[155]

On November 20, the weekly Brazilian magazine *Manchete* published a supposed interview with João Goulart concerning the grave economic problems of Brazil in which he called for "urgent and ample" reforms to prevent a "chaotic and subversive solution." In the article Goulart attacked groups that had not cooperated with him in his push for reforms and added that "if the government, in the fullness of its powers, had been in my hands alone (and I say this only as an illustration), no one could doubt that reforms would already have been accomplished." Goulart appealed to the Congress saying, "the word 'revolution' [is now] a real national threat. We must now take emergency measures in the field of internal and international finances, to retain the minimum of social tranquility, indispensable to the peaceful accomplishment of the structural changes which will make possible the realization of the historical destiny that awaits Brazil as a civilized and democratic nation."[156]

In the *Manchete* article, Goulart laid the blame for Brazil's economic crisis on the deteriorating terms of trade. He said that over half of Brazil's $3.8 billion debt was to become due by 1965 and that Brazil's capabilities coupled with the potential risks to the nation's stability "should give us [an] inalienable right to the credit we need."[157]

In reporting to the State Department about the *Manchete* article, Gordon noted with some concern that Goulart justified labor leaders intervening in larger political debates as a move to ensure the support of labor in his future policies. Gordon commented that Goulart "may be opening Pandora's box for [a] wave of strikes and labor agitation that could provide [a] basis for his assumption [of] extraordinary powers."[158]

Gordon continued to work with Carlos Alberto Carvalho Pinto, the finance minister. In October, Pinto introduced a plan requiring banks surpassing authorized credit limits to purchase treasury certificates from the Bank of Brazil. The purpose of this scheme was to finance the ailing Three Year Plan and simultaneously limit credit to the private sector. Private bankers protested, but the finance minister persevered.[159]

Pinto was planning another trip to Washington in early 1964 to negotiate with U.S. creditors. Brazil was the largest debtor of the Export-Import Bank, and the United States was urging that debt rescheduling for Brazil be done multilaterally with other creditors at the negotiating table. Pinto agreed but planned an initial negotiation with the United States to postpone payment on an Export-Import Bank note due on December 2. Gordon was worried that Goulart might proclaim a unilateral debt moratorium as some of his advisors were urging and encouraged the bank to consider Pinto's proposals. He commented that "with all his limitations, Pinto is on [the] side of [the] angels in this difficult situation; as [the] recent São Paulo meeting makes clear. I have no confidence that any successor picked by Goulart in his present frame of mind would be [an] improvement."[160]

Kennedy's Death: A Link Broken

Seemingly endless phone calls and people began coming in to the U.S. embassy on the afternoon of November 23, 1963, when the news reached Brazil that President Kennedy had been shot in Dallas. A line formed outside the embassy, and Gordon ordered the building kept open all night as people walked through and signed a book, paying respects to the assassinated U.S. president.[161]

Ambassador Campos was in Rio at the time seeking a decision on his proposed resignation, which he had submitted in August, but which had not been accepted. Campos was touched by the profound emotional reaction manifested in Brazil as a result of Kennedy's death. For Campos it "demonstrated by and large the antagonism towards the U.S. was more of a superficial political phenomenon."[162]

Goulart made a personal visit to the U.S. ambassador's home to pay his respects to the fallen president. For the Brazilian president, an important cord tying him to the United States had been cut. Goulart had admired Kennedy and had felt that he had enjoyed some rapport with the U.S. president. His visit to the United States had not become a foundation for consolidated collaboration between the two countries, but his personal meetings with Kennedy had tempered his natural bent for antagonism toward the United States and had provided Goulart with a personal link to that country. That relationship was now gone.[163]

A New Administration in Washington

Goulart sent President Lyndon Baines Johnson a letter of support and best wishes soon after Johnson became president. Goulart took the opportunity to add: "No economic system, however well conceived it may be, no modern technique, however effective it may be considered, can establish itself permanently or long assert its validity if it involves the sacrificing of human dignity." Goulart also spoke of the "spirit of reform" that would unquestionably be a vital part of Johnson's new administration and would "contribute to the fruitful cooperation that we must continue."[164]

A Rising Star

The first appointment Johnson made upon becoming president was that of fellow Texan, Thomas Mann, to be assistant secretary of state for interamerican affairs. Mann has been described as Lyndon Johnson's kind of person: "by almost unanimous consent, able, industrious, tough minded and knowledgeable, but . . . also uncommunicative . . . pragmatic."[165] Johnson publicly delegated to Mann unusual authority over U.S. Latin American policy, indicating that Mann was to be his "one voice" on hemispheric matters and giving him a simultaneous appointment as special assistant to the president. In addition, Mann was named coordinator of the Alliance for Progress.[166]

Johnson implied that his reason for concentrating such power in this one individual was that Mann was his longtime and trusted friend. Actually, political considerations played a fundamental role in this decision. By publicly delegating far-reaching responsibilities to Mann, Johnson took the control of Latin American policy out of the hands of Kennedy men and placed it with a career diplomat.[167]

U.S. Business and Military Policies

In late 1963, the Soviets apparently made an offer to provide transport planes to the Brazilian Air Force. That such plans might be underway was viewed as "extremely significant," and at the White House Gordon Chase communicated to McGeorge Bundy that "if such a deal seems to be happening, it would appear vital that we act quickly and vigorously. Among other things, we might want to consider the desirability of making a tough approach to the Russians."[168] Chase did not elaborate on what those "tough" measures might have been. As Ambassador Gordon had emphasized with Goulart, purchase of military equipment meant the establishment of training missions and ongoing contracts for spare parts with the providing country.[169] The United States had a strong Military Assistance Program (MAP) with Brazil and frowned upon any competition, particularly from the communist bloc.

Two days before his death, Kennedy had written David Rockefeller, president of the Chase Manhattan Bank, who together with other businessmen representing corporations with large interests in Latin America had recently formed the Business Group for Latin America (BGLA). One purpose of this group was to facilitate communication between the branches of government and the business community. Kennedy had assigned David Bell to coordinate governmental relations with the BGLA.[170] LBJ welcomed a meeting with the group early in 1964 and explained: "I want to take this opportunity to reaffirm the important role that private enterprise has to play in helping to achieve the goals of the Alliance for Progress."[171]

Brazil at Year's End: U.S. Perspective

It had been rumored that Goulart would replace Finance Minister Pinto with Leonel Brizola. Instead, when Pinto resigned at the end of 1963, Goulart appointed Ney Galvão, director of the Bank of Brazil and described by Thomas Skidmore as a "colorless bureaucrat." One of Galvão's first actions was to revoke the Pinto plan for selling treasury certificates to private banks that surpassed credit limits. The revocation of this controversial plan marked the end of any serious attempt to support the Three Year Plan.[172]

The Congress, fearing that Goulart might declare a state of siege while they were in recess, stayed in session over the Christmas holiday. As Gordon later remembered the progression of events—cabinets coming and going, the president's brother-in-law calling for people to arm themselves, attempted kidnappings—he recalled that Brazil took on an "unreal, Alice-in-Wonderland quality." Nineteen sixty-three had been a disappointing year from his perspective—the Bell-Dantas Agreement had failed and there had been extended settlement negotiations over expropriation (AMFORP was still being negotiated), and procommunist groups were gaining strength among students and the labor unions.[173]

Plots were growing for the deposition of Goulart—if he did not do away with the democratic process and assume extraordinary powers first. Gordon, during a Christmas vacation trip by car, learned that discontent extended even to small towns where scattered groups planned Goulart's ouster.[174]

To the ambassador, as the new year began, there seemed to be "only a 50/50 chance" of keeping things "on the rail." Gordon had a two-pronged policy: to try to maintain some equilibrium in Brazil (by assisting the finance minister with debt rescheduling) and to emphasize that it was Brazil and not the United States that was responsible for Brazil's current plight. In addition, Gordon and his staff tried to maintain a hand on the pulse not only of the official government, but also of the various conspirators who were discussing the overthrow of Goulart.[175]

A Profits-Remittance Law

To the ambassador's dismay, Goulart signed, in January 1964, the very restrictive Profits-Remittance Law that had been passed by the Congress in 1962.[176] The threat of this legislation becoming a law, coupled with runaway inflation and a volatile political climate, had almost dried up foreign investment in Brazil. To foreign investors, the most detrimental section of the Profits-Remittance Law concerned reinvested profits, which the law considered to

be national rather than foreign capital and which, therefore, could not be included in the capital base from which
profit remittances would be calculated.[177] Gordon, accompanied by Ambassador Campos, had had a special session
with Goulart, requesting that he veto the specific parts
of the law that were most restrictive to foreign investors.
That Goulart would sign the bill in full after having assured the ambassador he would do otherwise was another
indication to Gordon that he was dealing with a man
whose word could not be trusted. Gordon later remarked,
"He was like a cork bobbing in water. Goulart was impressed by the latest argument he heard."[178]

In his speech at the ceremony on January 17 at which
he signed the Profits-Remittance Law, Goulart denied accusations that he posed a threat to democratic order.
Goulart called his accusers the "same ones who planned
[the] *golpe* against [former president] Vargas and, more
recently, attempted [to] prevent me from assuming [the]
Presidency." Goulart explained, "Our dilemma is not one
of reform or *golpe* . . . we know that Brazil faces one sole
and true dilemma already defined by that young and great
statesman John Kennedy. The dilemma is: Reform or
Revolution."[179]

Further Overtures to the Left?

During the month of February the Brazilian foreign ministry announced that the Chinese People's Republic would
open a trade office in Brazil under an authorization
granted in 1961 by President Quadros.[180] Ambassador
Gordon, in accordance with U.S. standing policy, backed
the Taiwan-Chinese ambassador in discouraging the developing relationship between Brazil and the People's Republic of China. President Charles de Gaulle of France
had recently recognized the People's Republic, and Brazil's allowing that government to open a trade office was

viewed by the United States and others, in spite of denials by the foreign minister, as a prelude to Brazil's recognition of Communist China.[181]

Also in February, Ambassador Roberto Campos resigned his position and Jorge de Carvalho e Silva became chargé d'affaires ad interim at the Brazilian embassy in Washington, as Campos's replacement. Campos had found his ambassadorship in Washington a trying experience. He had been acutely aware that U.S. officials had been skeptical concerning his standing with the government of Brazil. Campos returned to Brazil convinced that he "should try to enter politics and acquire an independent political personality of [his] own."[182] In less than three months Campos would be offered the job of directing Brazil out of its economic turmoil as minister of planning and economic coordination under a new government.

Military Conspiracies

Search for a Leader

Small groups in the military had begun organizing against the government almost as soon as Goulart became president. Quadros's three former ministers, Denys, Moss, and Heck, were active among them.[183] General Olímpio Mourão Filho, "the diminutive fireball and longtime enemy of Goulart,"[184] headed the Fourth Army Division. He had one of the longest histories of plotting against President Goulart, but he was not the strong, respected leader needed to lead a coup against the government.[185]

The highly respected army chief of staff, General Humberto Castelo Branco, was disturbed by the economic and political direction of the Goulart administration and by the loss of discipline within the military. According to the former defense attaché Vernon Walters, some time after the first of the year—probably in early February 1964— Castelo Branco joined the conspirators and became their leader.[186]

Strengthening the U.S. Military Assistance Program

The U.S. embassy was apprised of developing conspiracies against the current government. If a showdown were to come, it seemed likely it would be between Goulart and a conglomeration of leftist and communist supporters (labor members, students, peasants, and noncommissioned officers in the military) on one side and on the other the military leadership aligned with traditionally conservative sectors (business, landowners) and a growing number of centrists to whom the Goulart administration appeared more and more ineffectual or dangerous.

The military was a traditional ally of the United States. War experiences served as a basis for continued shared weaponry and ongoing bonds of friendship. Further, the armed forces claimed the same enemy as the United States—communism. It was natural that Ambassador Gordon would wish to strengthen the capabilities of the U.S. ally, the military, particularly in light of the threat of a coup from either side.

In March 1964, Ambassador Gordon cabled the State Department (to the attention of Thomas Mann) and made a strong case for substantially increasing U.S. military aid to Brazil. He argued that the military was essential in the "strategy for restraining left wing excesses of [the] Goulart government," and he emphasized the role of the military in maintaining internal security that was critical in the climate of "growing social and political restlessness." Gordon noted that the underlying premise of the Military Assistance Program was to maintain the long-existing ties between the United States and Brazilian military and to develop closer links with the younger officers who might not feel an automatic alignment with the United States. Gordon played down the danger of a fascist-type military takeover, stating that if the events led to military intervention, he believed the armed forces "would be quick to restore constitutional institutions and return power to civilian hands."[187]

Beginning of the End

Friday the Thirteenth

On Friday, March 13, Ambassador Gordon left the embassy early in order to prepare for his flight from Rio to Washington late that evening. President Johnson had called a three-day conference of all U.S. ambassadors in Latin America beginning the following Monday.

March 13 was the day a much-heralded street meeting was to be held in the square located in front of the Dom Pedro II railway station and across from the war ministry in Rio de Janeiro. Goulart chose this site for the rally in hopes of augmenting the crowd with people going home from work. To counteract this, Carlos Lacerda declared a holiday for all workers in the state for that day.[188] In spite of those who might have stayed at home, the crowd in the square was between 120,000 and 200,000 according to one newspaper estimate.[189]

The speeches began at 5:00 P.M. One of the most inflammatory was delivered by Leonel Brizola who dramatically called for throwing out the Congress and for holding

a plebiscite "to install a Constitutional Assembly with a
view to creating a popular congress, made up of laborers,
peasants, sergeants, and nationalist officers, and authen-
tic men of the people."[190] The crowd responded wildly
with ovations and chants.

Goulart climaxed the evening with a speech which ran
for more than an hour. Earlier at the rally, it had been
announced that Goulart had signed a document (called the
SUPRA decree, after the abbreviation for Superintendency for Agrarian Reform Planning) for the expropriation of underutilized land ten kilometers on either side of
federal highways, railways, and water projects.[191] This
decree closely resembled a land reform idea of Goulart's
that Gordon had criticized months earlier.[192] When Goulart spoke of the SUPRA decree, the crowd responded
with enthusiasm. Goulart noted that this decree was not
yet agrarian reform, but only "a step forward on the path
of the great structural reform"[193] and that there would
be no structural reform without reforming the antiquated
constitution.[194]

At the rally, Goulart signed another decree, this one
expropriating all privately owned oil refineries, all of
which were already domestically owned, and putting
them under the control of Petrobrás, the federal monopoly. He also announced plans to sign another decree dealing with rent control and ceilings. The crowd cheered
these announcements as well.[195]

General Castelo Branco watched part of the rally from
across the street at the war ministry building. In the
opinion of Vernon Walters, Castelo Branco's decision to
overthrow Goulart was probably made as he watched and
listened to the crowd and the speeches calling for radical
reforms that attacked basic institutions and private ownership and demanded legalization of the Communist
party. Walters visited Castelo Branco that evening and

together they watched the mass meeting on television. Castelo Branco commented that the only signs he had seen at the rally were hammers and sickles. After hearing the speeches and watching the crowd's response, the general told his friend that he did not believe that Goulart would leave office when his term was completed.[196]

Ambassador Gordon watched the rally on television and listened to the last of Goulart's speech over the car radio on his way to the airport. He was disturbed by the unstable atmosphere, the overt communist participation in the rally, and the attacks on private ownership.[197]

Conference in Washington—A New Doctrine?

On Monday, March 16, the three-day conference began for U.S. ambassadors and some of the AID directors from Latin America. Ambassador Gordon was the only representative at the conference from the U.S. embassy in Brazil. Other participants were President Johnson, Secretary of State Rusk, Assistant Secretary Mann, AID Administrator David Bell, Attorney General Robert Kennedy, and representatives of various executive departments.[198]

President Johnson's speech on Monday reaffirmed strong U.S. support of the Alliance for Progress. He intended his remarks to allay any developing fears among Latin American leaders that U.S. interest in the Alliance, and therefore in Latin America, had waned with the change in administrations.[199]

Thomas Mann's address at a closed session on the evening of Tuesday, March 17, was leaked to the press and formed the basis of what became known as the Mann Doctrine. According to an article in the *New York Times*, Mann had outlined a policy in which the United States "would no longer seek to punish military juntas for overthrowing democratic regimes."[200] This policy seemed in effect to be a reversal of the Kennedy policy that had been "to deny diplomatic relations and economic aid to newly created military regimes, unless they offered firm assurances of restoring democratic rule within the foreseeable future." Mann was reported to have emphasized four purposes of U.S. policy in Latin America: support of economic growth, protection of U.S. investments, nonintervention, and opposition to communism. Mann allegedly told the ambassadors that each case would have to be decided on its own merits and that they "should be guided by pragmatism and diplomatic professionalism."[201]

Lincoln Gordon, who heard Mann's speech, thought that the press misrepresented Mann's views and that someone who did not like Mann had leaked the story.[202] Mann believes that the reason for the leak went back to the conflict between the Kennedy men and President Johnson and that he became the focus of attack because the authority delegated to him frustrated those who wished to continue to control United States–Latin American policy.[203]

Lincoln Gordon thought that news accounts of Mann's speech overstated a contrast by misrepresenting both the pre-existing Kennedy policy (making it sound more uniformly opposed to military coups) and the proposed LBJ policy (making Thomas Mann sound more sympathetic to such coups).[204] Gordon believes that Kennedy's dramatic show against military action in Peru did not help democratic institutions in that country and that in reacting to subsequent coups in Latin America, Kennedy had already shifted toward a more pragmatic approach.[205]

Vernon Walters corroborates Gordon on this count. When he was in Italy, just before transferring to Brazil, Walters had an occasion to talk with someone "high in the Kennedy administration" about the new assignment he

was soon to assume as defense attaché in Brazil. Walters
was told at that time that the United States was concerned about the political unrest and the growth of communism in Brazil, and that President Kennedy would not
be averse to seeing the overthrow of Goulart's government if it were replaced with a stable, anticommunist
government, aligned with the "free," Western world.[206]

Whether or not Tad Szulc's stories in the *New York
Times* provided an accurate report of Mann's description
of the United States–Latin American policy in the Kennedy and the Johnson administrations, the press account
was important. The Brazilian press picked up the story
and gave it heavy coverage. On Friday, March 20, *O Estado de São Paulo* reported that Thomas Mann had informed U.S. Latin American ambassadors of a new policy
according to which "military and right-wing dictatorships
will no longer be punished by non-recognition when they
overthrow democratic regimes." It further outlined
Mann's four principles as they had appeared in the *New
York Times*. The following day the headlines of *O Estado
de São Paulo* linked turnovers in the presidential staff
in the United States to the new policy toward Latin
America.[207] At least in Brazil, these changes were viewed
as both new and significant.

Rallies in Brazil—Washington Begins to Move

Factions in Brazil were becoming more polarized and
were mobilizing. In reaction to the rally in Rio on the
thirteenth, a "March of Family with God for Liberty"
was held in São Paulo on March 19. This march was
organized largely by women, and the banners were anti-
Goulart and anticommunist: "Resignation or Impeach-
ment" and "Down with Red Imperialism." There were
more presidential rallies and decrees planned.[208]

After the Washington conference adjourned, Gordon delayed his return to Brazil in order to confer with U.S. officials. A meeting about the Brazilian situation later that week included Secretary of State Dean Rusk, Secretary of Defense Robert McNamara, Director of the Central Intelligence Agency John McCone, Assistant Secretary of State for Interamerican Affairs Thomas Mann, Undersecretary of State George Ball, Special Assistant to the President Ralph Dungan, and Ambassador Gordon. Gordon was assigned to evaluate the situation in Brazil upon his return and to report back to Washington his opinion on conditions along with any policy suggestions he might have.[209]

Embassy Brainstorming

Ambassador Gordon returned to Rio on Palm Sunday, March 22. The following Monday, and most of Tuesday, he met with his top staff members to assess conditions in Brazil and to consider U.S. responses. Included in this planning group were Ambassador Gordon; Colonel Vernon Walters, defense attaché; Jack Kubisch, director of AID in Brazil; the CIA representatives; and Gordon Mein, deputy chief of mission. Also consulted were Niles Bond, consul general in São Paulo, and Robert Dean, who was in charge of the U.S. embassy branch in Brasilia.[210]

To the embassy group making the assessment, it appeared that Goulart's support of social and economic reforms was contrived and a thinly veiled vehicle to seize dictatorial power.[211]

The embassy planners considered that the United States had several options. It could take no new action and simply observe whether or not Goulart would attempt to extend his powers and, if he did, make the necessary adaptations thereafter. If this were the choice, the United States would continue the current policy of giving and withholding assistance and of supporting those groups most aligned with official U.S. policy goals.

In Ambassador Gordon's view, the best solution to the situation from both a Brazilian and a U.S. perspective would have been for Goulart to be "frightened off this campaign," for the presidential elections scheduled for October 1965 to be held, and for a new president to take office January 31, 1966. While Gordon did not completely reject the possibility that something might yet keep Goulart on this track, he believed that "Goulart's commitments to the revolutionary left [were then] so far-reaching . . . that the chances of achieving this peaceful outcome through Constitutional normalcy [seemed] a good deal less than 50/50."[212]

Defense Attaché Walters brought to the meeting on Monday morning a copy of a brief, as yet unpublished, memorandum he had just obtained, written by the army chief of staff, Castelo Branco, to the Army Officer Corps.[213] The memorandum provided a justification for the military in opposing the proposed constitutional assembly that Castelo Branco believed would lead to the closing of the Congress and the initiation of a dictatorship, and it upheld the charge of the military to defend and protect the constitution and the law.[214] In the Brazilian military, the memorandum was to serve as a catalyst for activating support for a challenge to Goulart's administration.

Walters informed the ambassador that General Castelo Branco had assumed active leadership in the theretofore widespread and loosely organized anti-Goulart movement.[215] U.S. intelligence indicated that a group of governors, including Carlos Lacerda of Guanabara, Adhemar de Barros of São Paulo, Ildo Meneghetti of Rio Grande do Sul, Nei Braga of Paraná, and José de Magalhães Pinto of Minas Gerais were aligning with this movement. The large showing of public support at the São Paulo march

and former President Kubitschek's recent acceptance of a
nomination for president served as rallying points in the
anti-Goulart movement.[216]

Gordon attempted to determine where Goulart's support was strongest and what that support might mean in
terms of strategies in the Goulart movement. The embassy believed Goulart was supported by 15 to 20 percent
of the population and of the Congress. Furthermore, Goulart and his supporters could enlist support from Petrobrás, the Department of Posts and Telegraphs, union
leadership in transportation and other trade unions, units
within the ministries of education and justice, elements
in other governmental agencies, and the civil and military
households of the president. Goulart could also find backing in rural workers' associations. The embassy believed
that attacks on military discipline, "through subversive
organization of the noncommissioned officers and enlisted
personnel," had had significant results—particularly in
the air force and the navy. Gordon and his sources, however, believed that the "overwhelming majority [of the
military] were legalist and anti-communist" and were
backed by a "modest minority of long-standing right-wing
coup supporters."[217]

Gordon believed Goulart would initially concentrate on
pressuring the Congress to pass reform measures including a plebiscite law, delegation of additional powers to the
president, legalization of the Communist party, and the
enfranchisement of illiterates. In order to achieve these
aims, Gordon foresaw Goulart's immediate tactics as including "a combination of urban street demonstrations,
threatened or actual strikes, sporadic rural violence,
and abuse of the enormous discretionary financial power
of the federal government . . . coupled with a series of
populist executive decrees of dubious legality." The embassy planners noted that Goulart could weaken resis-

tance at the state level by withholding federal financing, and they believed that he was already attempting to control the news media for propaganda purposes.[218]

The embassy assessment, based primarily on Walters' information, was that Castelo Branco preferred to make a coup after some obviously unconstitutional move by Goulart, but that Goulart might consciously avoid unconstitutional acts "while continuing to move toward an irreversible [de facto] . . . assumption of power." Based on this assumption, Gordon's understanding was that Castelo Branco was "therefore preparing for a possible move sparked by a communist-led general strike call, another sergeant's rebellion, a plebiscite opposed by Congress, or even a major government countermove against the democratic military or civilian leadership." The embassy concluded that if Castelo Branco moved against Goulart on an issue which was not clearly unconstitutional, the general would enlist political coverage from the governors or the Congress.[219]

After staff meetings and additional intelligence gathering, Gordon's assessment was that "a desperate lunge [by Goulart] for totalitarian power might be made at any time." Goulart planned further rallies and executive decrees. Gordon believed that any of those might become the forum for him to annul the Congress and the existing constitution and to establish a plebiscite to ratify both his action and a rewriting of the constitution.[220]

An attempt to overthrow Goulart was imminent. If the Brazilian military attempted a coup, a civil war appeared to be a real possibility. If events led to a showdown between these two forces, then the United States preferred that the anti-Goulart conspirators be successful in their bid for the government.[221]

Vernon Walters believed that the Brazilians would resent the United States' assuming a show of leadership in the coup. The conspirators had indicated that a coup was being planned and that if it were successful they were going to need economic cooperation and assistance from the United States in getting the government and the economy moving again. To this group the U.S. policy-makers had made no binding commitments but had left generally favorable impressions. As the United States considered alternative strategies, Walters recommended that no plans be made to send troops to Brazil.[222] Walters seemed to take care to avoid what might be interpreted as U.S. involvement in the developing conspiracy; he would drive past Castelo Branco's home without stopping to visit as he had in earlier, less difficult days.[223]

Embassy Recommendations

In the event that civil war broke out, the embassy task force developed two plans that could be used to tip the balance in favor of the side friendly to the United States (the anti-Goulart conspirators).[224]

The first plan dealt with petroleum supplies. In the event of a coup, access to petroleum could be critical to the conspirators, both for military transportation and to keep civilian aspects of the country running smoothly. The U.S. planners feared that Goulart supporters in the Petrobrás union might blow up the refineries.[225] If U.S. petroleum were needed and supplied, the United States could in this one action be helpful both to the conspirators and to Brazil as a whole, since presumbly large portions of the country might otherwise be temporarily paralyzed without oil supplies.[226]

The second plan proposed by the embassy was that a U.S. carrier task force be sent to Brazil. Two purposes could be served through this action. Based on reports from various intelligence sources, the embassy planners believed that when the coup occurred the largest section of the country would probably fall immediately to Castelo Branco, but that a dissident fringe might resist, particularly in Rio Grande do Sul and Pernambuco. A U.S. carrier fleet in waters off the Brazilian coast might assist in maintaining stability through a U.S. military presence. The carriers might also be used to evacuate U.S. citizens if the military coup developed into a life-threatening situation.[227]

On March 27, Ambassador Gordon sent a lengthy Top Secret teletyped message to the State Department that he requested be passed immediately to Secretary of State Rusk, Assistant Secretary Mann, Director of the Office of Brazilian Affairs Ralph Burton, Defense Secretary McNamara, Assistant Secretary of Defense McNaughton, Chairman of the Joint Chiefs of Staff General Maxwell Taylor, CIA Director John McCone, Colonel J. C. King, Desmond Fitzgerald (CIA), McGeorge Bundy (White House), Ralph Dungan (White House), and General Andrew P. O'Meara (U.S. commander in chief-south, Canal Zone).[228]

In this message, only parts of which have been declassified, the ambassador concluded that Goulart was definitely engaged in a campaign to seize dictatorial powers and that, if Goulart were to succeed in this effort, Brazil would probably come "under full communist control." Gordon flatly rejected the possibility that Goulart's purpose might be to secure constructive social and economic reform but proposed instead that it was "to discredit the existing constitution and the Congress, laying a foundation for a coup from the top down." Gordon described Goulart's tactics, the resistance led by General Castelo Branco, and the conditions under which Castelo Branco would move. The ambassador believed that "the possibilities clearly included civil war, with some horizontal or vertical division within the Armed Forces, aggravated by widespread possession of arms in civilian hands on both sides."[229] Gordon recommended the two contingency plans developed at the embassy that would keep open U.S. options to be able to respond positively in favor of the conspirators.[230]

Sailors Rebel

On March 26, around 1,200 sailors rallied at the metal workers' union building in protest of Navy Minister Mota's ordering the arrest of eleven men in the sailors' union who had been making demands for political privileges and improved living conditions. When the rally did not disband, Goulart flew in from Rio Grande do Sul on March 27 to intercede. Labor leaders were involved in the negotiations, and the sailors were granted amnesty. Goulart accepted Mota's resignation over the incident and selected as a replacement retired Admiral Paulo Mario Cunha Rodriguez, whose name had been suggested by the Comando Geral dos Trabalhadores (CGT). It was a galling affront to the military that leftist and communist leaning labor leadership should give direction to military affairs.[231]

When General Kruel conveyed to Goulart the detrimental impact on the president's relations with the military of the actions he had taken in the case of the sailors' rebellion, the president reacted verbally with concern. Any positive action by the president was short-circuited by the reassurances of Assis Brasil, head of the presidential military household, that Goulart did indeed have strong military backing. Goulart once again suffered for being poorly informed.[232]

On March 30, Goulart delivered an impassioned televised speech before 2,000 army corporals and sergeants at Rio's Automobile Club. Goulart had been advised by former Prime Minister Tancredo Neves of the folly of his addressing a military group so soon after granting the sailors amnesty, but Goulart was confident he could carry the evening. Casting aside his prepared speech, Goulart aligned himself with the rebellious sailors. The president accused a privileged minority with responsibility for the crisis in Brazil. Goulart talked of false discipline and vowed that he would not allow disorder in the name of order.[233]

The Armies Move

The coup "began" in Minas Gerais. On March 30, Governor Magalhães Pinto issued a manifesto denouncing the Goulart government and supporting the military's right to fight for the "glorious destiny assigned to them by [the] constitution."[234]

General Mourão Filho, commander of the Fourth Military Region located in Minas Gerais, heard Goulart's March 30 speech on the radio and decided to act. The morning of Tuesday, March 31, he began moving troops and tanks toward Rio. Castelo Branco was surprised and concerned because all of the coordinating plans had not been completed. Unable to stop Mourão's advance, even temporarily, Castelo Branco and the other conspirators focused on giving Mourão all possible support.[235]

That same day, General Kruel urged Goulart by phone to make a turnabout on his leftist policies. The president, citing his popular support, refused. That evening Kruel ordered his army to move on Rio, thereby joining "*a revolução*."[236]

U.S. Activities

Communications Stepped Up

As developments in Brazil reached a crisis, the Americans stepped up the efficiency of their communications. A teletype machine, set up in the embassy during the week after Gordon returned from Washington, remained in operation through part of the first week in April, with exchanges between the State Department and the Rio embassy usually scheduled at least twice daily.[237] On the afternoon of March 30, Secretary Rusk instructed the U.S. embassy in Brazil to expedite dissemination of information by including the White House, the office of the secretary of defense, the Joint Chiefs of Staff, the commander in chief of the southern command, and the CIA as recipients of "all important telegrams dealing with substantive matters."[238] Washington took a further lead. A cable that evening from Secretary Rusk (drafted by Burton and approved by Mann) instructed all U.S. consulates in Brazil to be on a twenty-four–hour alert and to report directly to Washington "any significant developments involving military or political resistance to the Goulart regime."[239] Ambassador Gordon canceled a trip to Alagoas at the suggestion of Vernon Walters who was convinced the coup would begin on the thirty-first.[240]

On the evening of March 30, Niles Bond, consul general in São Paulo, cabled Washington that "two sources active in [the] anti-Goulart movement say that [the] coup against GOB [government of Brazil] should come within forty-eight hours." Bond was not convinced about the forty-eight–hour timetable but believed that the opposition to Goulart was taking the offensive. Bond added an important message: these two unnamed principal conspirators had inquired for the first time "whether [the] American fleet can reach Southern Brazil fast."[241]

On the evening of March 30, the Associated Press released a House Foreign Affairs Committee Report dealing
with "Winning the Cold War." The story, while reporting
criticism of Goulart's tolerance of communism, quoted the
report as saying that "despite [the] critical situation
[in] Brazil, there is little prospect for [a] communist takeover there in the foreseeable future." Concerned about
the timing of positive statements about Goulart just as the
United States was committing itself to his overthrow,
Secretary Rusk gave a special briefing to reporters to
explain that the report had been prepared in January
and that Brazil was "increasingly subject to communist
influence," much to the dismay of the United States.
The briefing statements were reported along with the
story.[242] Gordon was pleased and felt it was timely for
the United States to make "some public expression of
interest and concern."[243]

At 11:30 A.M. on March 31 in Washington, a meeting
was held attended by Secretary Rusk and other State
Department representatives, Defense Secretary Robert
McNamara, Chairman of the Joint Chiefs of Staff Gen.
Maxwell Taylor, U.S. Commander in Chief of Southern
Forces (USCINCSO) Lt. Gen. Andrew P. O'Meara, CIA
Director John McCone, and other top officials. At the
meeting there were briefings on the military situation in
Brazil and on U.S. naval and air support capabilities. The
group considered what political actions should be taken
(such as consultation with other Latin American coun-
tries, public statements, and other possibilities) and discussed organizational arrangements for dealing with the
Brazilian crisis, including setting up an interdepartmental
task force and considering "relations and communications
between [the U.S.] Embassy [in] Rio, consulates, and
U.S. military forces."[244]

At this meeting or earlier a military contingency plan
was considered and approved that went beyond the embassy's two suggestions that petroleum and a carrier fleet

be sent to Brazil. This third plan involved arrangements for actual arms and ammunition to be sent to Brazil as contingency support for the conspirators.[245]

After the Washington meeting, Undersecretary Ball, Assistant Secretary Mann, and Special Assistant to the President Ralph Dungan prepared a teletyped message to Ambassador Gordon. The message stated, "the dilemma we face is: a) our concern not to let an opportunity pass that may not recur, b) our concern not to get USG [U.S. government] out in front on [a] losing cause." The tele-type suggested that Gordon send no more messages to Brazilian governors or military until some policy decisions were made in Washington.[246]

Earlier Gordon had sent word to some governors in Brazil, in which he had emphasized the necessity from the U.S. point of view of creating a government which would have a claim to legitimacy.[247] The teletype message from the State Department suggested that some combination of four items would be regarded by the United States as minimal elements in a claim to legitimacy: "establishment of unconstitutional acts by Goulart," a "claim to [the] Presidency by [the] individual in [the] line of succession," "action by Congress or some elements of Congress having some claim to legislative authority," and "recognition or ratification by some or all state governments." Although only Mourão's army was in revolt, the teletype made clear what conditions would be necessary for any overt assistance by the United States to the group laying claim to the government after the overthrow of Goulart: "the formation of a government claiming to be [the] Govern-ment of Brazil," "the establishment of some color of legiti-macy," "the successful seizure and holding of significant Brazilian territory in the name of such government," "and a request by such government to the United States and other American States for recognition and assistance

in upholding [the] Constitutional government." The teletype did ask what civilians might lay claim to the presidency but added "this does not rule out [the] possibility
of [a] military junta as [a] last resort, but that would make
U.S. assistance much more difficult."[248]

The teletype of March 31 contained some specific questions about Brazilian military plans for action and then
turned to the logistics of getting petroleum, oil, and lubricants (called POL in teletype communications) to Brazil.
The message indicated that tankers could not arrive for
fourteen days. An alternative suggested by Washington
was the possibility of delivering the petroleum, oil, and
lubricants by air; such a delivery, however, would require
a "secure landing field able to accept jets and [the] prob-
able need for fighter cover during transit to Brazil" or
"alternatively and preferably [the] use of West Coast
group which would involve landing and over-flight rights
over other American states." The second alternative assumed the establishment of a new government that would
be recognized by the countries the craft would fly over.[249]

On the morning of March 31, former President Kubitschek indicated that there would be resistance to a takeover in the form of a general strike lasting two or three
days but that workers would return to work "when they
got hungry."[250] Based on U.S. policy makers's concerns
that there might be a two- or three-day general strike,
Gordon was asked in the March 31 teletype whether it
would be "necessary for the U.S. to mount [a] large material program to assure [the] success of [the] takeover."[251]

Plans into Action

The afternoon of March 31, the United States began turning military contingency plans into action. The first plan
implemented sent a heavy attack aircraft carrier, the

Forrestal, and supporting destroyers (including one destroyer with guided missiles) sailing toward Brazilian waters. The purpose of the task group was "to establish U.S. presence in this area and to be prepared to carry out tasks as may be assigned."[252] The ships were to depart Norfolk, Virginia, at 7:00 A.M. local time (9:00 A.M. Rio time) on April 1 and were scheduled to arrive at Santos, São Paulo's port, around April 11. Additional support for the ships included attack oilers, ammunition ships, and provision ships.[253]

Meanwhile, Maj. Gen. George S. Brown was appointed mission commander for project "Brother Sam." This operation combined the carrier task force and POL support planned at the Rio embassy with the contingency operation, which originated in Washington, to supply arms and ammunition to the military conspirators in Brazil.[254]

The Joint Chiefs of Staff instructed U.S. Commander in Chief South Lt. Gen. Andrew P. O'Meara to airlift 250 twelve-gauge shotguns marked "Brother Sam" to Ramey Air Force Base in Puerto Rico by 3:00 P.M. Rio time on April 1.[255] In addition, 110 tons of small arms and ammunition marked "Brother Sam" were to arrive no later than noon EST on April 1 at McGuire Air Force Base, N.J., for airlifting to Brazil.[256] Planes for the airlift included 7 C135 transport aircraft, 8 fighter aircraft, up to 8 tanker aircraft (for air rescue support), 1 communications aircraft, and 1 airborne command post.[257]

The Joint Chiefs of Staff emphasized secrecy in "Brother Sam" instructions that four tankers be loaded with a total of 136,000 barrels of motor gas, 272,000 barrels of JP-4 (jet fuel), 87,000 barrels of aviation gas, 33,000 barrels of diesel, and 20,000 barrels of kerosene. The ships were due at Aruba by 7:00 P.M. Rio time on March 31 where the petroleum, oil, and lubricants would be loaded.[258]

U.S. Tracking

During the day of March 31, former President Kubitschek issued an ambiguous statement to the press and radio in which he said there was "still time to save the peace and legality by reestablishing discipline and the chain of command for love of country, of Brazilians and of God."[259] Gordon considered this statement an optimistic sign and communicated to Washington that if he were able to see Kubitschek that evening, he would "of course pump him on [the] reasons [for] his optimism."[260]

Gordon did meet with Kubitschek at the former president's home at about 9:00 P.M. that evening. Gordon wanted Kubitschek to take a stronger position against Goulart and to use his considerable influence to "swing [a] large congressional group and thereby influence [the] legitimacy issue."[261] Kubitschek felt that the legitimacy problem that so concerned Gordon would be readily handled by the Congress, if there were a favorable military balance. The former president was distracted by the lack of news from São Paulo (Kruel had not yet marched) and kept flipping dials on his radio. Kubitschek explained that a move from São Paulo was critical because if Mourão's rebellion were quashed, "Goulart would be on [a] high road to dictatorship." When Gordon left Kruel still had not made his move.[262]

At 11:00 P.M. on the thirty-first, Colonel Walters went to the apartment of Gen. Floriano de Lima Brayner.[263] Walters explained that Ambassador Gordon wanted to know about the situation in Brazil. Brayner told Walters that Kruel had issued his manifesto. "Graças a Deus," responded the American colonel.[264]

At 7:00 A.M. at Howard Air Force Base in Panama (9:00 A.M. Rio time) on April 1, a Top Secret joint U.S. Army–Navy–Air Force–CIA task force went into action under the command of air force Major General Breitweiser.[265]

The purpose of this task force appears to have been to follow and coordinate the logistics of Brother Sam.[266]

Brazilian Requests

A naval group headed by Admiral Levi Reis set up a command post on Copacabana Beach on the morning of April 1. He was trying to arrange for three destroyers to operate off Rio and a submarine to operate off Santos as part of the coordinated anti-Goulart movement. Reis asked the U.S. chief of naval mission "if and when U.S. might be able to provide fuel for submarines."[267]

At 10:00 A.M. on April 1, U.S. officials in Washington contemplated the political effects of overt U.S. support in the coup and asked the embassy whether "the momentum [would] continue on the anti-Goulart side without some covert or overt encouragement from our side?" The concern of the policy makers appears to have been not the appropriateness of U.S. involvement in the internal affairs of Brazil, but whether overt indication of U.S. support would "play into Goulart's hands at this moment?"[268]

Gordon responded, "Momentum now clearly gathered and for these hours does not need special encouragement from us. . . . At this moment overt indication [of] our support would be a serious political error which would play into Goulart's hands." Gordon did not rule out overt U.S. support, for he added, "We shall of course continue focusing on this question hourly as situation evolves." To Washington's question of whether any leaders in the rebellion had "pressed . . . for overt support," the ambassador played down the importance of the requests of Governor Adhemar de Barros and others from São Paulo "who continue talking unclearly about arms needs and possible desirability of [a] show of Naval Force." In the meantime, U.S. contingency operations continued moving

toward their positions of support to the overthrow of
Goulart.[269]

U.S. Information

U.S. decision making was based on accurate and timely
information from excellent intelligence sources. An unnamed source in the telegraph agency informed the embassy when Second Army troops crossed the state line
between São Paulo and Rio de Janeiro on the morning
of April 1.[270] There were two demonstrations that afternoon in downtown Rio, and runners shuttled back and
forth between these rallies and the embassy keeping the
staff apprised.[271] Vernon Walters made arrangements to
see Castelo Branco or a member of his staff at 2:00 P.M.
on April 1 and again on the morning of April 2.[272]

In the early morning hours of April 1, the president of
the Brazilian Senate, Auro de Moura Andrade, without a
congressional vote declared the Brazilian presidency
vacant. The president of the supreme court, without a
vote of that court, presided over the swearing-in of an
interim president, Paschoal Ranieri Mazzilli, president of
the Chamber of Deputies.[273]

Goulart's support was disoriented and ineffective.
Strikes were called but were not carried out. The resis-
tance lacked coherent planning and strong leadership. At
about 1:00 P.M. on April 1, Goulart left Rio, flying to
Brasilia.[274] Instead of taking a planned stand in Brasilia,
Goulart flew on to Rio Grande do Sul that night.

On the afternoon of April 1, Gordon and his staff were
in the ambassador's eighth-floor embassy office tracking
movements by radio, telephone, and messengers. In spite
of the day's heat, the air conditioning was cut off as a
precaution against someone's using the vents to smoke
out the occupants. The drapes were closed to discourage

snipers.[275] Events were moving quickly. Castelo Branco had issued a statement that Goulart had stepped outside legal bounds.[276] The First and Second armies reached an agreement without fighting. Word came that the anticoup demonstrations in Rio had dispersed and that most resistance appeared to have been neutralized.[277]

U.S. Geared for Assistance

At 5:30 P.M. Gordon teletyped the State Department, "We believe it is all over, with [the] democratic rebellion already 95% successful." He noted that there might yet be some civil strife and that "we have begun staff work on possible needs for internal security help, financial stabilization, etc."[278] Washington responded, "We have [had] a special task force here now at work several days on economic and financial assistance, emergency relief, etc. and are prepared promptly to act on your recommendations." After the teletype conference, Undersecretary Ball called President Johnson to tell him the news.[279]

Overt U.S. military support of Goulart's overthrow quickly became unnecessary. Gordon cabled Washington a lengthy situation report at 1:00 A.M. on April 2, in which he described the strengths of the apparent victors and the few remaining pockets of resistance. In considering possible U.S. responses, he noted that "until democratic[280] control [of] refineries [is] assured, [the] possible need for petroleum products cannot be excluded." This statement meant that the tankers loaded with petroleum, oil, and lubricants continued toward Brazil. Gordon did not immediately cancel the pending shipment of 110 tons of U.S. arms and ammunition, because, he explained, "until [the] Third Army situation [is] clearly under control, . . . we cannot completely exclude [a] possible request for materiel." Gordon focused on the potential economic repercussions of the coup and communicated to Washington that he believed that the situation might "require some emergency supplies such as food, public safety materiel, POL." He went on to say that "we are also considering here what many economic aid steps will be required to provide rapid support to [the] new administration."[281]

Although the embassy staff began to focus on economic support, they maintained their high-level intelligence of military operations in Brazil. On April 2, at 4:00 P.M., Gordon communicated to Washington that he had "just received confirmation from Castelo Branco that all resistance has ceased in Porto Alegre and democratic forces now in full control of RGS [Rio Grande do Sul]. This eliminates last pocket military resistance."[282]

That same afternoon, 200,000 persons crowded into downtown Rio for a victory parade of the group March of Family with God for Liberty. Gordon described the euphoria of the crowd waving Brazilian flags and anticommunist banners, singing their national anthem, and throwing confetti. Gordon added that the "only unfortunate note was [the] obviously limited participation in [the] march of lower classes."[283]

U.S. attention was largely focused on changing the economic picture for Brazil. On April 2, in the day's first teletype message, Gordon was asked who he thought would be the next finance minister and what the chances were that he would in the next thirty days make a serious effort to put Brazil's financial affairs in order.[284]

On the evening of April 2, Assistant Secretary Mann described to Gordon the thinking at the State Department concerning U.S. assistance to Brazil, which, according to Mann, would have two objectives: to be helpful to and support the new regime and to encourage a "reasonable stabilization development program supported by total free world resources, including U.S." Mann explained that in order to get either U.S. congressional or international agency support, "it will be necessary to prevail upon the Brazilian authorities to work out a program for economic development and financial stability." The United States hoped a program of this sort would begin immediately under Interim President Mazzilli. Mann noted that attention must be given to the unattractive aspects of any effective program which could be "exposed to attack from many sides, particularly the communist and commie-liners."[285]

The assistant secretary added that "in light of latest developments" the ambassador might wish to consider areas in which the U.S. government could cooperate more effectively with the Brazilian government; Mann mentioned specifically Title I/PL 480 (Food for Peace) shipments, development of the Northeast, agrarian reform, and reconsideration of the current U.S. position to provide only project, as opposed to program, loans. Mann indicated that the United States was interested in seeing a presidential successor "above party interests," a strong finance minister and cabinet that would implement an effective economic program, and an economic package that would require "sacrifice for all groups including land reform and more effective tax collection." Mann inquired of the ambassador, "To what extent could [the] possibility [of] large scale external assistance influence along [the] lines of this message?"[286]

Additional U.S. assistance to Brazil of the magnitude being considered would require congressional approval. On April 2, Gordon sent a cable by way of the State Department and White House to Carl Hayden, president pro tempore of the Senate and a member of the Senate Appropriations Committee, recommending that "the greatest possible consideration be given to any request [by the new Brazilian government] for economic emergency assistance." Gordon described Goulart's "de facto ouster" as "a great victory for [the] free world," without which the result could have been a "total loss to [the] West of all

South American Republics." Gordon indicated that the
change in government should "create a greatly improved
climate for private investments" and for the Alliance for
Progress. Noting that AID had been important to the
economic and political life of Brazil in "strengthening efforts in support of democratic ideals," Gordon closed,
"I believe it to be to U.S. interests to support and
strengthen as much as possible the present regime."[287]

Recognition Strategies

The ambassador wanted President Johnson to issue a
recognition statement as soon as the Brazilians had clari-
fied and acted upon a plan for presidential succession. In
the meantime, he cautioned Washington, "suggest avoid-
ance [of a] jubilant posture."[288]

The Brazilian constitution provides automatic forfeiture
of office if the president leaves the country without congressional permission. Goulart, however, had still been in
the country when Mazzilli had been sworn in; therefore,
there was no constitutional basis for this unilateral move.
Gordon was troubled by the illegitimacy of the new government and wanted the Brazilian Congress to ratify the
action by vote before President Johnson sent a message of
recognition. With that purpose in mind, he advised Bob
Dean, who headed the U.S. embassy branch in Brasilia,
to seek out congressional legitimization.[289]

In the meantime, Ambassador Gordon and Undersecretary Ball had a series of teletyped conversations concerning the wording of the recognition message to be sent
from President Johnson.[290] Gordon's draft contained
the phrase "in accordance with Constitutional procedures."[291] Gordon wished to use the opportunity to emphasize obliquely that the United States expected the new
government to proceed along constitutional lines.[292] Ball
deleted the line, and Gordon suggested an alternative re-

ferring to Mazzilli's "installation as constitutional President of Brazil."[293] Ball vetoed this wording also. His rationale for leaving out both suggestions was possibly because he thought they were clumsily worded[294] or possibly because he thought an earlier reference to Brazil's resolving difficulties "within a framework of constitutional democracy"[295] made the suggestion unnecessary[296] or perhaps it was because it seemed foolish to call a procedure constitutional when in fact Interim President Mazzilli had been appointed illegally.

There was further discussion on the timing of Johnson's message. Ambassador Gordon recommended that the statement of recognition be issued immediately. At 6:00 P.M. on April 2 he sent a teletype to Washington emphasizing that "despite continued uncertainty [of the] whereabouts of Goulart I reiterate [my] recommendation [that the] Presidential message [be sent]." Ball was willing to acquiesce to the ambassador's recommendation pending the removal of the "constitutional" phrases, but he had some misgivings as to whether or not the statement might be premature or whether such alacrity might be interpreted as U.S. interference in the internal affairs of another nation. The issue here appears not to be concern that the United States might be overextending its involvement, but rather that it might be interpreted as such. Gordon made his case for immediate release of Johnson's statement:

> We naturally reflected on precisely these points before making [our] recommendations. Since [the] country [is] now completely pacified and in [the] hands [of] democratic forces with Congressional support even though no formal vote, I cannot see how the message could be construed as interference. Since prospects [for a] Congressional vote now seem minimal, I believe that the sooner we act the better. Our failure to send [the] message by tomorrow would

begin to raise questions here [in Brazil] as to whether we are reacting as in Peruvian case. Our line should be that there is no break in constitutional continuity.[297]

Johnson's message was released that night, less than eighteen hours after Mazzilli's hurried installation. The U.S. president sent his "warmest good wishes," admiring "the resolute will of the Brazilian community to resolve . . . difficulties within a framework of constitutional democracy and without civil strife." Johnson looked forward to "intensified cooperation in the interests of economic progress and social justice for all, and of hemispheric and world peace."[298]

The next day (April 3) Secretary Rusk adroitly obfuscated the issues that had been troubling U.S. policy makers. In reply to questions at a news conference, he stated the U.S. position:

I would think that recognition is basically a political act which normally, in the usual circumstances, applies where a government is in control of the country and accepts its international responsibilities, but this will vary from time to time because as a political act it needs to be taken alongside of the other interests of the United States in a particular situation, including our interest in moving jointly with others whenever possible in a concert of policy. Now in the case of Brazil, of course, this matter does not arise because the succession there occurred as foreseen by the Constitution and we would assume that recognition is not involved in that particular issue or point.[299]

Goulart finally left Brazil on April 4 and flew to Uruguay to join his family in exile. Before he left Brazil, Secretary Rusk cabled the U.S. embassy in Montevideo communicating his concern that Goulart might be received

as if he were still Brazil's president on the grounds that
he had not yet resigned. Rusk suggested to the U.S. staff
in Montevideo "it would be useful if you could quietly
bring to the attention [of] appropriate officials the fact
that despite his allegations to [the] contrary Goulart has
abandoned his office."[300]

Closing Down Military Contingency Plans

By noon on April 2, the ambassador was contemplating
canceling the orders of the carrier task force sailing toward Brazil. The next afternoon, through orders of Admiral Harold Smith, this operation was canceled with instructions to "preserve the 'Quick Kick' cover story for
entire operations." Smith suggested that the carrier force
carry out a training exercise on April 8 "off MHC" and
then revert units to normal operations.[301] On the afternoon of April 3, General O'Meara in Panama, under whom
the joint task force had been tracking all military contingency operations for Brazil,[302] recommended that the
"110-ton package of arms and ammunition continue to be
held at McGuire pending Ambassador Gordon's deter-
mination of whether Brazilian military forces or state
police forces will require early U.S. support," and that
the Tactical Air Command, the Strategic Air Command,
and the Military Air Transport Service sections of the
"Brother Sam" operation be released, and that "only that
part of the POL movement which [the] Ambassador con-
siders essential to current situation be continued."[303]

The "Brother Sam" petroleum, oil, and lubricants remained in transit until Friday or Saturday, April 4 or 5,
when Ambassador Gordon contacted officials at Petrobrás
to see if Brazil had need of extra petroleum products. The
Brazilian officials thanked the ambassador but declined
the offer. Gordon reported to Washington that the petroleum, oil, and lubricants would not be needed, and these
supplies were diverted elsewhere.[304]

On the evening of April 3 an order from the Joint Chiefs of Staff canceled the airlift and fighter and tanker support for the "Brother Sam" arms and ammunition project.[305] The actual materiel remained in storage until Monday, April 7, when the Joint Chiefs of Staff directed that the arms order pending shipment to Brazil be canceled and that the guns be returned to normal storage.[306]

Thus, the "Brother Sam" military contingency plans initiated action and terminated it, with the United States never having been physically involved in Goulart's overthrow.

Political Perspectives on U.S. Economic Assistance to Brazil

Economic assistance is a major tool of U.S. foreign policy. In 1961, the Alliance for Progress marked a dramatic increase in total U.S. economic assistance to Brazil (see Tables 1 and 2).

Development assistance loans through AID during this period were divided into two categories: program and project.[307] Central governments are recipients of program loans that are made for general economic development and address macro-economic problems involving a country's balance-of-payments deficit and its fiscal and monetary programs. The United States tends to prefer multilateral solutions to problems requiring program loans, so that cooperation with the IMF is usually sought in program loans. Project loans are more specific in purpose, such as for construction of a dam or road. Some U.S. assistance is in the form of grants; with the self-help goals in the Alliance for Progress, however, U.S. policy tended to emphasize loans.

Table 1

U.S. Loans and Grants to Brazil, 1946–1974

(Millions of dollars, by U.S. fiscal years)

	U.S. Overseas Loans and Grants— Obligations and Loan Authorizations					
Program	Postwar Relief Period	Marshall Plan Period	Mutual Security Act Period	Foreign Assistance Act Period		
	1946–1948	1949–1952	1953–1961	1962–1965	1966	1967
I. *Economic Assistance*[a]*—total*	19.9	5.4	314.2	954.5	329.0	240.0
Loans	16.3	—	180.5	727.9	258.4	199.0
Grants	3.6	5.4	133.7	226.7	70.6	41.0
a. *AID and predecessor agencies* ..	—	2.6	50.3	586.0	243.7	214.9
Loans	—	—	0.5	523.0	229.3	199.0
Grants	—	2.6	49.8	63.0	14.4	15.9
(Security supporting assistance)	(—)	(—)	(—)	(75.5)	(—)	(—)
b. *Food for Peace (PL 480)*	—	—	241.4	295.9	79.1	21.6
Title I-total	—	—	220.0	191.4	29.1	—
Repayable in U.S. dollars— loans	—	—	—	—	29.1	—
Payable in foreign currency— planned for country use ..	—	—	220.0	191.4	—	—
(Total sales agreements, incl. U.S. uses)	(—)	(—)	(262.8)	(240.6)	(—)	(—)
Title II-total	—	—	21.4	104.5	50.0	21.6
Emergency relief, economic development, & world food	—	—	—	37.9	33.5	9.3
Voluntary relief agencies ...	—	—	21.4	66.6	16.5	12.3
c. *Other economic assistance*	19.9	2.8	22.5	72.6	6.2	3.5
Peace Corps	—	—	—	11.1	6.2	3.5
Other[c]	19.9	2.8	22.5	61.5	—	—
II. *Military Assistance—total*	—	—	170.6	108.4	30.6	32.6
Credits or loans	—	—	—	23.4	11.6	18.4
Grants	—	—	170.6	84.9	19.0	14.2
a. MAP grants	—	—	121.2	64.9	17.3	12.2
b. Credit sales under FMS	—	—	—	23.4	11.6	18.4
c. Military assistance service- funded (MASF) grants	—	—	—	—	—	—
d. Transfers from excess stocks ...	—	—	22.6	2.9	1.7	0.5
e. Other grants	—	—	26.8	17.1	—	1.5
III. *Total Economic and Military Assistance*	19.9	5.4	484.8	1,062.9	359.6	272.6
Loans	16.3	—	180.5	751.3	270.0	217.4
Grants	3.6	5.4	304.3	311.7	89.6	55.2
Other U.S. government loans and grants	54.0	104.5	996.8	6.0	16.9	30.0
a. Export-Import Bank loans	54.0	104.5	996.8[d]	6.0[d]	16.9	30.0
b. All other[e]	—	—	—	—	—	—

Source: U.S. Agency for International Development, Office of Financial Management, Statistics and Reports Division, "U.S. Overseas Loans and Grants" [Washington, D.C., 1974].
* Less than $50,000.
[a] Official Development Assistance (ODA): Official concessional aid for development purposes.
[b] Capitalized interest on previous-year loans. Total includes $9.2 million in capitalized interest on previous-year loans.
[c] Includes $22.5 million Surplus Property Credits and $16.4 million Defense Mobilization

U.S. Overseas Loans and Grants—
Obligations and Loan Authorizations

		Foreign Assistance Act Period					Total FAA Period 1962–1974	Total Loans and Grants 1946–1974	Repayments and Interest 1946–1974	Total less Repayments and Interest
1968	1969	1970	1971	1972	1973	1974				
280.7	29.2	154.0	117.6	21.0	53.8	17.2	2,197.0	2,431.1	226.5	2,204.6
243.7	3.1	95.0	90.8	2.1	33.3	1.0	1,654.3	1,760.5	226.5	1,534.0
37.0	26.1	59.0	26.8	18.9	20.5	16.2	542.8	670.7	—	670.7
193.8	12.4	88.0	79.4	12.1	40.6	5.0	1,475.9	1,422.7	84.0	1,338.7
180.9	*	75.0	67.5	2.1ᵇ	33.2	1.0	1,311.0	1,220.3ᵇ	84.0	1,136.3
12.9	12.4	13.0	11.9	10.0	7.4	4.0	164.9	202.4	—	202.4
(—)	(—)	(—)	(—)	(—)	(—)	(—)	(75.5)	(75.5)		
82.9	10.2	62.4	35.1	5.7	9.6	6.2	608.7	850.7	68.0	782.7
62.7	—	19.9	23.3	—	—	—	326.4	547.0	68.0	479.0
62.7	—	19.9	23.3	—	—	—	135.0	135.6	47.5	88.1
—	—	—	—	—	—	—	191.4	411.4	20.5	390.9
(—)	(—)	(—)	(—)	(—)	(—)	(—)	(240.6)	(503.4)	(—)	(503.4)
20.2	10.2	42.5	11.8	5.7	9.6	6.2	282.3	303.7	—	303.7
9.7	2.4	35.0	3.8	—	4.9	4.1	140.6	140.6	—	140.6
10.5	7.8	7.5	8.0	5.7	4.7	2.1	141.7	163.1	—	163.1
4.0	6.6	3.6	3.1	3.2	3.6	6.0	112.4	157.7	74.5	83.2
3.9	3.5	3.5	3.1	2.9	2.6	4.2	44.5	44.6	—	44.6
0.1	3.1	0.1	—	0.3	1.0	1.8	67.9	113.1	74.5	38.6
36.1	0.8	0.8	12.1	20.8	17.6	52.7	312.4	482.7	71.1	411.6
18.5	—	—	9.4	20.0	15.0	51.7	168.0	168.1	71.1	97.0
17.6	0.8	0.8	2.7	0.8	2.6	1.0	144.4	314.6	—	314.6
2.6	0.8	0.8	0.8	0.8	0.7	1.0	101.9	222.8	—	222.8
18.5	—	—	9.4	20.0	15.0	51.7	168.0	168.1	71.1	97.0
—	—	—	—	—	—	—	—	—	—	—
0.1	—	—	—	—	—	—	5.2	27.7	—	27.7
14.9	—	—	1.9	—	1.9	—	37.3	64.1	—	64.1
316.8	30.0	154.8	129.7	41.8	71.4	69.9	2,509.4	2,913.8	297.6	2,616.2
262.2	3.1	95.0	100.2	22.1	48.3	52.7	1,822.3	1,928.6	297.6	1,631.0
54.6	26.9	59.8	29.5	19.7	23.1	17.2	687.2	985.3	—	985.3
66.6	27.9	63.2	75.0	301.3	145.7	326.7	1,059.3	2,244.3	1,573.8	670.5
50.8	27.9	63.2	75.0	299.8	142.3	325.7	1,037.6	2,224.1	1,555.3	668.8
15.8	—	—	—	1.5	3.4	1.0	21.7	20.2	18.5	1.7

Development; loans under the Social Progress Trust Fund, $61.5 million; Institute of Interamerican Affairs, $6.4 million; and other programs, $6.3 million. FY 1974 data represents grants under the Interamerican Foundation, $1.6 million and International Narcotics Control (State) $0.2 million.
ᵈ Excludes refunding of $292.2 million in FY 1961; $85.6 million in FY 1964; and $6.6 million in FY 1965.
ᵉ Includes $4.8 million in direct loans from Overseas Private Investment Corporation (OPIC).

Table 2

U.S. Loans and Grants to Brazil, Fiscal Years 1955–1965

(Millions of dollars, by U.S. fiscal years)

Program	1955	1956	1957
I. *Economic Assistance*[a]*—total*	5.8	39.7	121.3
Loans	0.3	30.7	79.3
Grants	5.5	9.0	42.0
a. *AID and predecessor agencies*	3.0	3.6	4.5
Loans	—	—	—
Grants	3.0	3.6	4.5
(Security supporting assistance)	(—)	(—)	(—)
b. *Food for Peace (PL 480)*	2.5	35.6	110.2
Title I—total	—	30.2	108.3
Repayable in U.S. dollars—loans	—	—	—
Payable in foreign currency—planned for country use	—	30.2	108.3
(Total sales agreements, incl. U.S. uses) .	(—)	(39.7)	(127.3)
Title II—total	2.5	5.4	1.9
Emergency relief, economic development, & world food	—	—	—
Voluntary relief agencies	2.5	5.4	1.9
c. *Other Economic Assistance*	0.3	0.5	6.6
Contributions to international lending org.	—	—	—
Peace Corps	—	—	—
Other	0.3	0.5	6.6
II. *Military Assistance—total*	13.4	8.0	18.4
Credits or loans	—	—	—
Grants	13.4	8.0	18.4
a. MAP grants	12.7	7.8	8.3
b. Credit sales under FMS	—	—	—
c. Military assistance service-funded (MASF) grants ..	—	—	—
d. Transfers from excess stocks	0.7	0.2	*
e. Other grants	—	—	10.1
III. *Total Economic and Military Assistance*	19.2	47.7	139.7
Loans	0.3	30.7	79.3
Grants	18.9	17.0	60.4
Other U.S. government loans and grants	49.8	56.0	193.2
a. Export-Import Bank loans	49.8	56.0	193.2
b. All other	—	—	—

Source: U.S. Agency for International Development, Office of Financial Management, Statistics and Reports Division, "U.S. Overseas Loans and Grants" [Washington, D.C., 1974].
General Note: Details may not add to totals because of rounding.
*Less than $50,000.

1958	1959	1960	1961	1962	1963	1964	1965	Total 1955–1965
9.1	11.9	13.4	92.2	205.5	141.3	336.9	270.8	1,247.9
—	0.5	—	54.6	154.1	92.1	254.8	226.9	893.3
9.1	11.4	13.4	37.6	51.5	49.2	82.1	43.9	354.7
5.5	8.9	11.6	7.5	85.1	86.5	179.5	234.9	630.6
—	0.5	—	—	74.5	62.9	165.4	220.2	523.5
5.5	8.4	11.6	7.5	10.6	23.6	14.1	14.7	107.1
(—)	(—)	(—)	(—)	(—)	(25.5)	(50.0)	(—)	(75.5)
3.6	3.0	1.8	84.7	72.5	47.9	150.9	24.6	537.3
—	—	—	81.5	44.0	32.0	115.4	—	411.4
—	—	—	—	—	—	—	—	—
—	—	—	81.5	44.0	32.0	115.4	—	411.4
(—)	(—)	(—)	(95.8)	(55.0)	(40.7)	(144.9)	(—)	(503.4)
3.6	3.0	1.8	3.2	28.5	15.9	35.5	24.6	125.9
—	—	—	—	21.7	0.3	9.6	6.3	37.9
3.6	3.0	1.8	3.2	6.8	15.6	25.9	18.3	88.0
—	*	*	—	47.9	6.9	6.5	11.3	80.0
—	—	—	—	0.9	1.6	4.0	4.6	11.1
—	*	*	—	47.0[b]	5.3[b]	2.5[b]	6.7[b]	68.9
19.1	20.4	27.1	24.3	44.4	17.9	34.1	12.0	239.1
—	—	—	—	—	—	23.4	—	23.4
19.1	20.4	27.1	24.3	44.4	17.9	10.7	11.9	215.6
18.2	11.7	18.1	23.9	26.8	16.7	10.3	11.1	165.6
—	—	—	—	—	—	23.4	—	23.4
0.9	0.2	0.8	0.4	0.5	1.2	0.4	0.8	6.1
—	8.5	8.2	—	17.1	—	—	—	43.9
28.2	32.3	40.5	116.5	249.9	159.2	371.0	282.8	1,487.0
—	0.5	—	54.6	154.1	92.1	278.2	226.9	916.7
28.2	31.8	40.5	61.9	95.9	67.1	92.8	55.8	570.3
17.5	122.2	6.8	188.3	—	—	—	6.0	639.8
17.5	122.2	6.8	188.3	—	—	—	6.0	639.8

[a] Official Development Assistance (ODA): Official concessional aid for development purposes. The United States sharply increased its economic loans and grants to Latin American countries beginning with President Kennedy's announcement of the Alliance for Progress on March 13, 1961.
[b] These are loans from the Social Progress Trust Fund.

Any U.S. development loan or grant has to meet standards for potential contribution to development and for feasibility. During the early sixties, AID funded a variety of projects in Brazil, including health services, educational services, roads, and power plants. Ambassador Gordon, a respected economist, worked with the various finance ministers to assist in creating sound economic and development policies within the social and economic development design of the Alliance for Progress.[308]

Bilateral aid generally has an implied if not an overt political purpose. During the sixties a pattern emerged from the U.S. aid programs to Brazil of assistance being withheld from those who were perceived as friendly with the radical left or with communists and of aid being channeled most often to those governors and institutions that were perceived as protectors of a noncommunist society. This pattern has suggested to some that the United States exerted an undue influence on the direction of internal Brazilian affairs.

In the April 19, 1964, edition of *O Estado de São Paulo*, Assistant Secretary Thomas Mann described the pattern and purposes of U.S. assistance before and after the coup:

> Last January when we assumed our duties we were convinced that communism would rapidly erode the government of João Goulart in Brazil. Even before assuming our actual position, moreover, we already were following a policy destined to grant aid to certain state governments in Brazil. We did not furnish any money to support the balance of payments or the budget, nor did we take any measures that could directly benefit the central government of Brazil. In our opinion, which I believe is shared by many Brazilian specialists, and in words attributed to efficient governors of various states, the limited assistance destined for the Goulart administration contributed toward financing democracy. . . . Now after the re-

placement of Sr. Goulart, if the government of Brazil supports a stabilization and self-help program, which is the type of development program that we want to see, or in other words, if they accept their responsibilities in the Alliance for Progress, we would be prepared to consider making appreciably more substantial funds available.[309]

Mann later elaborated on this statement: the United States did not "intervene in Brazil's internal affairs" in the classic sense of the word (military coercion), and he did not recall that the United States tried to influence Brazil's policies through economic leverages.[310] On this point, State Department cables written by Mann and his later recollections tend to create divergent impressions.[311]

U.S. economic assistance during the Goulart administration evolved into one of not assisting the central government. Ambassador Gordon denies the contention that U.S. aid was designed to harm the central government or that it was purposely skewed to assist Brazilian opposition to Goulart. He asserts that the policy of giving aid to "islands of administrative sanity," which met Alliance for Progress standards, was designed for the most part, though not entirely, for economic development purposes.[312]

There were no program loans negotiated while Goulart was president.[313] As a result of the Bell-Dantas negotiations, there was a final release of $25.5 million in April 1963 of monies from a program loan negotiated during the Quadros administration.[314]

In June 1964, three months after the coup, the United States negotiated and released $50 million as "an emergency measure to meet a foreign exchange crisis." Within four years there were four program loans for an additional total of $475 million from the United States to the military government of Brazil.[315] U.S. policy makers could point to the fiscal inconsistencies in the Goulart administration in order to justify both not releasing funds to his government and subsequent generosity of the U.S. government to the military that overthrew Goulart.

Based on State Department work sheets and the annual reports to Congress it is difficult to draw conclusions about the ideological or security purposes of U.S. project assistance. Reports do indicate that between 1956 and 1970 the only years in which the United States gave project loans directly to state governments or state-owned enterprises were the calendar years 1962 to 1966 (see Table 3).[316] Loans, however, could benefit more than one state; and, aside from knowledge of a governor's political affiliations, the political implications of funding one group over another require further specific knowledge (through cables, memoranda, interviews, or other studies) of the negotiations and the options available.

President Kennedy's request to AID Administrator Fowler Hamilton to do something favorable for Brazil before their October 1962 elections, which the United States considered crucial, carried obvious political implications.[317] The United States unsuccessfully tried to influence the gubernatorial race in Pernambuco in those October elections by funding projects of those opposing Miguel Arraes, a nationalist and social reformer who was regarded by the United States as a communist.[318]

Riordan Roett, in his book *The Politics of Foreign Aid,* analyzes the political constraints and purposes which permeated the large AID mission to the Brazilian Northeast in the early sixties. Roett describes numerous decisions made by AID officials for the stated purpose of regional development that were designed first to meet the more immediate objective of blocking communist penetration in the area. The United States concentrated on high visibility programs that would gain support from the governors and that would prove that noncommunist democratic government responded to the needs of the people. Roett

Table 3

U.S. Project Loans by Receiving Brazilian Entity, 1956–1970

TOTAL LOANS

Calendar Year	Dollars	Cruzeiros	Combined
1956		$ 14,529,653.32	$ 14,529,653.32
1959	$ 227,451.76		227,451.76
1961			
1962	2,982,669.95	24,321,167.19	27,303,837.14
1963	29,029,881.19	20,257,947.96	49,287,829.15
1964	108,619,051.76	87,674,565.34	196,293,617.30
1965	78,845,470.22	51,897,605.74	130,743,075.96
1966	65,600,000.00	3,672,360.94	69,272,360.94
1967	50,317,000.00	2,592,264.36	52,909,264.36
1968	10,700,000.00		10,700,000.00
1969	65,200,000.00		65,200,000.00
1970	15,400,000.00		15,400,000.00
Total	426,921,524.88	204,945,565.05	631,867,089.93

FEDERAL GOVERNMENT

Calendar Year	Dollars	Cruzeiros	Combined
1956		$ 14,529,653.32	$ 14,529,653.32
1959			
1961			
1962		24,321,167.19	24,321,167.19
1963		18,551,396.91	18,551,396.91
1964	$ 40,309,043.69	60,553,602.67	100,862,646.36
1965		393,819.47	393,819.47
1966	1,400,000.00	3,672,360.94	5,072,360.94
1967	8,400,000.00		8,400,000.00
1968	10,700,000.00		10,700,000.00
1969	37,800,000.00		37,800,000.00
1970	15,400,000.00		15,400,000.00
Total	144,009,043.69	122,022,000.50	236,031,044.19

FEDERALLY OWNED ENTERPRISES

Calendar Year	Dollars	Cruzeiros	Combined
1956			
1959			
1961			
1962			
1963			
1964	$ 748,764.75		$ 748,764.75
1965	1,960,000.00		1,960,000.00
1966	13,175,000.00		13,175,000.00
1967	41,917,000.00		41,917,000.00
1968			
1969			
1970			
Total	57,800,764.75		57,800,764.75

STATE GOVERNMENTS

Calendar Year	Dollars	Cruzeiros	Combined
1956			
1959			
1961			
1962			
1963		$ 1,706,551.05	$ 1,706,551.05
1964	$ 15,900,000.00	19,690,973.65	35,590,973.65
1965	12,900,000.00	26,254,635.54	39,154,635.54
1966	20,000,000.00		20,000,000.00
1967			
1968			
1969			
1970			
Total	48,800,000.00	47,652,160.24	96,452,160.24

STATE-OWNED ENTERPRISES

Calendar Year	Dollars	Cruzeiros	Combined
1956			
1959			
1961			
1962	$ 2,982,669.95		$ 2,982,669.95
1963	7,614,879.49		7,614,879.49
1964	4,293,561.00		4,293,561.00
1965	11,400,000.00	$ 23,953,675.56	35,353,675.56
1966			
1967			
1968			
1969			
1970			
Total	26,291,110.44	23,953,675.56	50,244,786.00

PRIVATE ENTERPRISES

Calendar Year	Dollars	Cruzeiros	Combined
1956			
1959	$ 227,451.76		$ 227,451.76
1961			
1962			
1963	21,415,001.70		21,415,001.70
1964	12,192,682.32	$ 7,429,989.22	19,622,671.54
1965	41,097,343.68	1,295,474.17	42,392,818.85
1966	14,800,000.00		14,800,000.00
1967		2,592,264.36	2,592,264.36
1968			
1969			
1970			
Total	89,732,479.46	11,317,782.75	101,050,208.21

PRIVATE AND GOVERNMENTAL OWNERSHIP (MIXED)			
Calendar Year	Dollars	Cruzeiros	Combined
1956			
1959			
1961			
1962			
1963			
1964	$ 35,175,000.00		$ 35,175,000.00
1965	11,488,126.54		11,488,126.54
1966	16,225,000.00		16,225,000.00
1967			
1968			
1969	27,400,000.00		27,400,000.00
1970			
Total	90,288,126.54		90,288,126.54

Source: U.S. Senate, Committee on Foreign Relations, Subcommittee on Western Hemisphere Affairs, *United States Policies and Programs in Brazil*, pp. 189–191.

demonstrates the political implications of U.S. development loan activities by comparing the concentration of U.S. economic assistance to the Northeast before the coup (when the anticommunist security issue was critical) with the neglect of those projects after the coup and the concomitant economic support of the new central government, which then assumed the primary role in the opposition to communism.[319]

Some U.S. economic assistance in the sixties supported projects that corresponded to the desire of the United States to see Brazil take serious measures to deal with problems of internal security. The purpose of the AID Public Safety Program was to improve the quality of the police forces in Brazil. In the early sixties, in addition to criminology equipment, this AID program furnished Brazilian police with over 31,000 grenades, as well as batons, body shields, and vests for riot control. Trainees studied such subjects as riot control, fire arms, investigations, counterintelligence, handling explosives, patrol operations, and border and customs control.[320] Compared to total AID monies in Brazil, the Public Safety Program

was relatively small; it is, however, an example of how
U.S. assistance was able to address a political concern
for internal security matters in the country through an
economic development program.

Not all economic assistance is through development aid
programs. Throughout the fifties and the sixties, Brazil
was by far the largest single recipient of the U.S. Military
Assistance Program (MAP) in Latin America.[321] Military
assistance to Brazil during the Goulart administration
fluctuated between $17 million and $44 million annually
(see Table 1).

Ambassador Gordon recognized the MAP as a "major
vehicle for establishing close relationships with personnel
of [the] armed forces" and as "a highly important factor
[in] influencing [the Brazilian] military to be pro-U.S." He
regarded the Brazilian military as "an essential factor
. . . in [the] strategy for restraining left-wing excesses of
the Goulart government." While Brazilian police forces
were important in maintaining order against minor distur-
bances and crime prevention, the ambassador viewed the
regular armed forces as the "only force capable of putting
down large-scale uprisings or disorders."[322] Judging from
State Department cables, the United States considered
internal security in Brazil a significant purpose and focus
of the MAP.

In addition to outright military assistance and the Public Safety Program, Brazil received "security supporting
assistance" channeled through AID during the year before the coup ($25 million) and the year of the coup ($50
million). Security supporting assistance does not have to
meet the same requirements as development assistance
loans and grants and is associated with some perceived
threat to U.S. security.

Lincoln Gordon was a particularly able ambassador. His
suggestion that no policy is so perfectly orchestrated that
the United States completely controls the outcome of a

series of events rings true. Taken individually, no loan or grant proves that U.S. development programs in Brazil were politically designed. Taken as a whole, however, U.S. development assistance, as well as military aid, seems to have had security motives of creating and maintaining U.S. alliances and of eradicating communism from the hemisphere. For the United States there was no conflict. The *Foreign Assistance Report to the Congress for 1962* specifically linked social justice and economic development with a stand against communist subversion and infiltration. For Brazilians, such as SUDENE Director Celso Furtado or President Goulart, this black-and-white model was sometimes politically unfeasible. U.S. policy makers reacted to this lack of cooperation by assuming an adversary position and by seeking friendships and alliances elsewhere.

What was the role of U.S. economic assistance in the events in Brazil in the early sixties? The Goulart years were a disappointment for Ambassador Gordon in the lack of recognizable accomplishments through economic aid from and collaboration with the United States by Brazil.[323] The accomplishments of specific projects could not eradicate a dismal set of economic trends in that country up to 1964. The evidence does not suggest that U.S. economic assistance caused the downfall of Goulart. There is evidence that U.S. aid further weakened an already weak central government, not only by withholding assistance from Goulart's government which the U.S. policy makers felt would not or could not handle the aid responsibly, but also by effectively bypassing that government through direct U.S. dealings with and support of other groups, leaders, and institutions in the country and by frequently aligning U.S. assistance with those elements of Brazilian society that eventually overthrew Goulart.

It is not necessary to conclude that U.S. development aid should be given regardless of the validity of the domestic economy. It must be recognized, however, that U.S. development assistance can contribute in many ways to the success or failure of that domestic economy. The evidence suggests that in Brazil political issues perceived by the United States as threatening its own national security structured decisions that were justified in terms of development. This statement raises questions of what development is, what authority a government should have in structuring its own development goals, and what role U.S. assistance can and should play in the economic and social development of another nation.

CONCLUSION

In a democracy there are institutions that protect individual freedoms against the potential tyrannies of government. The viability of these institutions is more important in safeguarding democracy than are the actions of any individual who occupies a place of leadership in that democracy. In the nineteen sixties, it became apparent to U.S. leaders that democratic institutions could not survive without a concern for social welfare and economic development. The Alliance for Progress was an attempt to have a coherent policy in Latin America that might respond to these concerns from within a democratic framework. When respect for democratic institutions collided with more accepted notions of self-interest and national security, however, words and action diverged with action on the side of self-interest. Thus, the U.S. government aligned itself with the military coup of 1964.

The stated U.S. policy toward Brazil under President Goulart, in the beginning, was to try "to encourage him [Goulart] to believe that cooperation with the United States [was] to his and Brazil's advantage."[324] U.S. officials went about this task in numerous ways. Total U.S. economic and military assistance jumped from $41 million in 1960 to $117 million in 1961 to $250 million in 1962. At the same time, the United States withheld release of Export-Import Bank loans, to cover Brazil's growing national debt, pending specific austerity measures on the part of the Goulart government. President Kennedy invited Goulart to Washington and laid the groundwork for a personal relationship between the two presidents. When problems arose for businessmen in Brazil, Ambas-

sador Gordon and his staff stood ready to act as liaisons
between the disagreeing parties.

As these more established avenues of diplomatic relations failed to achieve the desired cooperative spirit in
Brazil, U.S. diplomats made efforts to influence the internal workings of the Brazilian political system. Officials
at the State Department told Ambassador Campos that
through Robert Kennedy's visit they hoped to affect Goulart's cabinet choices. The U.S. embassy disbursed funds
in support of certain candidates in the October 1962 elections. The following year one U.S. consul suggested
forming student organizations or pressure groups outside
official Brazilian government sanctions that could serve
as a base for anticommunist students. The large military
assistance program was considered important in generat-
ing a pro-U.S. posture by that group, which was, in turn,
considered critical in the "strategy for restraining the
left-wing excesses of the Goulart government."[325]

One result of these actions is that it raised the question
of how far U.S. diplomats might go to encourage Brazilian
cooperation, thus granting that U.S. policy makers would
attempt to influence the internal working of Brazil's political system. The question became one of degree: what
amount and type of pressure were American officials willing to bring to bear on political events in Brazil?

As a result of U.S. policies and alliances during Goulart's presidency, the United States became tied to a military government that has increasingly maintained its
authority by force and repression.[326] The discrepancy between policy rhetoric, and action earned the United
States strong criticism and laid it open to attack by some
who would attribute the Brazilian coup to U.S. direction.[327] Documents declassified to date do not, in fact, cor-
roborate this allegation.

There is no evidence that the United States instigated,
planned, directed, or participated in the execution of

the 1964 coup. Each of these functions seems to have
been in the hands of Castelo Branco and his fellow officers.
At the same time, ample evidence suggests that the
United States approved of and backed the military overthrow of Goulart almost from the time of the plot's in-
ception. The United States reinforced its support by developing military contingency plans that could be useful
to the conspirators should the need have arisen.

Good military strategy prepares for all contingencies.
The Brazilian conspirators had an ally in the United
States, but it was in the best interest of both the United
States and the generals that the coup, if possible, run
under Brazilian steam. The United States could be depended upon to act with discretion, a fact attested to by
Vernon Walters' discontinued practice of making social
calls at the home of Castelo Branco during the period
before the coup.

Messages between the embassy and Washington officials indicate that the United States was well informed
of conspiracy plans and strategies. Circumstantial evidence suggests that the United States did not resort to
second-guessing for designing the size, scope, and purpose of its contingency support plans. Cables document
that Walters was in daily contact with Castelo Branco and
other military leaders. That the United States was willing
to coordinate with the Brazilians is reinforced by the ambassador's contacting federal Petrobrás officials before
canceling the U.S. POL operation.

This is not to deny that Ambassador Gordon was surprised at the timing of the coup, as he claimed to have
been. Niles Bond's forty-eight–hour warning and Vernon
Walter's process of elimination notwithstanding, indications are that Mourão also surprised his fellow generals
when he began his march on the thirty-first, and that
Castelo Branco had planned for the revolution to begin
two days later.

U.S. policy makers did not wish to attach the United States to some splinter group that had little chance of success. All planned U.S. support was of a marginal nature. The coup was expected to be a Brazilian movement with U.S. materiel and presence available if needed to tip the balance. Hence Washington's initial hesitation on March 31 when only General Mourão was moving. Once Mourão's march became "the revolution," the cables indicate that full U.S. government backing was available.

The United States was not involved in the execution of the coup only because there was no need to be. Two weeks after the coup, Ambassador Gordon wrote Special Assistant to the President Ralph Dungan, "The best kind of contingency planning is always the kind that need not be put into practice, but it was very comforting for us to know that we would not have been helpless in the event of a less happy outcome."[328] Thus the ambassador's later statement that the coup had been a "100% purely Brazilian movement," and that "neither the American Embassy nor I personally played any part in the process whatsoever,"[329] while true, tends to obfuscate the scope of U.S. policy makers' intent, commitment, and activities in the events of March and April 1964.

U.S. officials appear to view U.S. interests in Latin America as being served if those nations do not pose a strategic military threat to the United States or block U.S. economic activity. To encourage the prevalence of these interests, U.S. policy makers can apply economic incentives, political pressure, and, if need be and as a last resort, military force.

In Brazil in the early sixties, U.S. policy makers applied economic leverage by giving and withdrawing U.S. aid from the central government. The tight rein that the United States maintained on its program assistance to the central government was justified by economic standards, but economic justification was inextricably entwined with political motivation. The embassy eventually limited U.S. assistance to "islands of administrative sanity" that were "aligned with the purposes of the Alliance for Progress," and were viewed as bulwarks against the threat of communism in Brazil. The effect, if not the purpose, was further to weaken the central government by fragmenting its control over the states.

Ambassador Gordon has argued that the central government had to approve any U.S. assistance in Brazil. This policy may have kept the central government informed of U.S. assistance, and perhaps of potential political alignments; but it diffused Brazil's development planning away from the central government toward state governments and agencies and the United States. The argument that the central government retained veto power is weakened by the political infeasibility of the central government's denying generous assistance to state or private entities for worthwhile projects and because the central government was able to offer little alternative funding.

Leaders must have some source of power. This power may come through popular mandate, congressional backing, or military control; or it can come from some outside source, such as the United States. Goulart was a weak president—that is, aside from any personal lack of leadership ability, he lacked organized political support. The parliamentary restrictions were a reminder to him of his general lack of strength in the military, the Congress, or with any of Brazil's traditional power elites, and from the time of his inauguration the United States viewed him as suspect. Goulart attempted to manipulate military promotions to his benefit, but in view of events it would appear that this tactic did not bring the desired result of strong backing by the armed forces. Rather, it caused a split in the military and eventually contributed to Goulart's overthrow.

Few economic leverages were available to Goulart to
rally support behind his presidency; and, while the measures being encouraged by the United States might have
been economically sound, they would have been politically
unpopular. From this position of weakness Goulart would
not, or could not, initiate needed austerity measures.
Goulart's vehicle for marshalling support was to create
a spirit of nationalism and to call for structural reforms
that might enlarge his popular base. The tactics of the
United States were demeaning to President Goulart and
tended both to attack his personal pride and to undermine
his appeal for national pride. Goulart's reaction was to
rebel and turn to labor, his only traditional source of
political backing. He attempted to use this strength in
labor, as well as among students and noncommissioned
military, as a springboard for expanding his power base.

In an analysis of U.S. policy, it seems important to
consider not only the actions taken by U.S. policy makers,
but also those not taken. One area not documented is what
the implicit effect was of U.S. officials being friendly with
those who were actively plotting to overthrow the government. U.S. officials went to some lengths to express
their concern at the threat of the growth of the political
left in trade unions and student groups and the potential
these groups might have for contributing to a seizure of
the government by Goulart. It appears that those same
officials did not feel led to express a similar concern at
the prospect of a military overthrow of the constitutional
government. One might conclude from events in Brazil
that U.S. officials look with less concern at a break in the
constitutional order if it is perpetrated by that group with
whom they are most friendly (in this case, the military
as opposed to the president or political leftists or communist sympathizers).

U.S. cables and memoranda in 1964 refer to those who
plotted to overthrow Goulart as the "democratic forces."

There seems to have been no conflict in the minds of U.S. officials over someone's believing in the democratic process and at the same time plotting to overthrow a constitutional democracy, albeit a weak one, by military force. In retrospect, an interesting question to ask these officials would be what the grounds were for calling this group "the democratic forces."

That U.S. officials felt some alliance with those who seized control of the Brazilian government on April 1, 1964, is reflected in their corresponding activities supporting the military ouster of Goulart. Indications are that U.S. policy makers believed and hoped that Brazil would quickly return to civilian control. The U.S. government cast its lot with the military conspirators, and the generosity of subsequent U.S. aid to the military regime indicates that, by and large, U.S. leaders considered U.S. interests better served by the generals than by Goulart.

NOTES

Abbreviations Used

ACSI: Assistant Chief of Staff for Intelligence
AFCIN: Air Force Commander-in-Chief
CINCLANT: Commander-in-Chief, Atlantic Forces
CINCLANTFLT: Commander-in-Chief, Atlantic Fleet
CFB: Country File, Brazil
COMSECONDFLT: Commander of the Second Fleet
COMUSARSO: Commander U.S. Army, Southern
   Forces
CSA: Chief of Staff, Army
CSAF: Chief of Staff, Air Force
DNI: Director of Naval Intelligence
JANAF: Joint Army, Navy, Air Force
JCS: Joint Chiefs of Staff
JFK: John F. Kennedy Presidential Library, Waltham,
   Massachusetts
LBJ: Lyndon Baines Johnson Presidential Library,
   Austin, Texas
NSF: National Security File
POF: Presidential Office Files
USCINCSO: U.S. Commander-in-Chief, Southern
   Forces
WHCF: White House Central Files

Notes on References to Materials in the Presidential Libraries

When citing material from the presidential libraries, I have included the following information whenever possible: the name of the originator of the document, the recipient of the document, the date, the file name, the box and folder titles, and the library in which the document is found. When this information was incomplete, I state in the note what my best judgement is regarding the source or date and I identify the document by the number assigned by the library.

Military messages are relayed using "date-time group" based on Greenwich mean time (also known as "Zulu," commonly and in this book, denoted by a Z). Date-time groups are read as follows: the first two digits are the day of the month. Z time is five hours ahead of time in Washington, D.C., and three hours ahead of Rio de Janeiro, São Paulo, and Brasilia time. Thus, 010230Z April would be read as April 1, 2:30 A.M. Greenwich mean time. This notation would refer to March 31, 9:30 P.M. Washington time. The advantage of using standard time becomes more evident as the time of the coup approaches and the sequence of events becomes critical.

1. Ambassador Lincoln Gordon to Secretary of State Dean Rusk, 10 April 1964, CFB Vol. 3, NSF, LBJ; also, U.S. Senate, Committee on Foreign Relations, *Nomination of Lincoln Gordon of Massachusetts to be Assistant Secretary of State for Interamerican Affairs*, pp. 34–35, 37. In 1966, before the Senate Committee on Foreign Relations, which was considering his nomination as assistant secretary of state for interamerican affairs, Ambassador Lincoln Gordon said, "I am absolutely convinced that the principal purpose for the Brazilian revolution of March 31 and April 1, 1964, was to preserve and not destroy

Brazil's democracy, and I believe the record since that time bears that out" (p. 8). Although a series of institutional acts preempted the rights of individuals and placed unprecedented powers in the hands of the military presidents, Gordon held to this statement, in spite of the "exceptional powers" of the postcoup regime, until 1968 when the Fifth Institutional Act was signed. That act marked the abandonment of all legal pretense of upholding democratic institutions and gave the president virtually absolute authority. The president immediately suspended the Congress and there was a wave of arrests to counter political dissension. The Fifth Institutional Act prompted Gordon to sign a letter of protest over the arbitrary use of power in Brazil (Lincoln Gordon interview, January 19, 1976, Washington, D.C.).

2. Many of the documents at the Johnson Library have been translated into Portuguese by Marcos Sa Correa, *1964 Visto e Comentado pela Casa Branca*.

3. There are recent publications that cite primary sources now open to scholars in Brazil. See John W. F. Dulles, *Castello Branco*, and Moniz Bandeira, *O Governo João Goulart*.

4. U.S. Department of State, "Declaration of the Peoples of America" and "Charter of Punta del Este," in *American Foreign Policy Current Documents, 1961*, pp. 393–409.

5. "Charter of Punta del Este," pp. 398–409.

6. "Goulart," Box 112, Goulart Visit, POF, JFK; see also Thomas E. Skidmore, *Politics in Brazil, 1930–1964*, p. 114.

7. "Current Intelligence Memorandum: Brazilian President João Goulart," March 30, 1962, Box 12, POF, JFK; Skidmore, *Politics in Brazil*, pp. 129–130.

8. Skidmore, *Politics in Brazil*, p. 114; see also Vernon A. Walters, *Silent Missions*, p. 379.

9. Gordon interview, January 19, 1976.

10. Roberto de Oliveira Campos interview with John E. Reilly, p. 34.

11. JCS to White House, Attn: Gen. Clifton, August 28, 1961, Box 12 and 13, Brazil Vol. 1, NSF, JFK.

12. Quoted in John W. F. Dulles, *Unrest in Brazil*, pp. 149–150; Skidmore, *Politics in Brazil*, pp. 204–209.

13. Skidmore, *Politics in Brazil*, pp. 204–212.

14. Gordon interview, January 19, 1976.

15. "Background Paper: Brazil," Attachment to Memorandum from L. P. Battle to Richard N. Goodwin, September 14, 1961, Box 112, Brazil, Security, 1961, POF, JFK.

16. Ibid.

17. Gordon interview, January 19, 1976.

18. Ibid.

19. Campos interview, p. 17.

20. Ibid., pp. 17–18.

21. "Notes on Questions Concerning Brazil Which Most Preoccupy U.S. Opinions," Box 112, Goulart Visit, POF, JFK.

22. Skidmore, *Politics in Brazil*, p. 271.

23. "Position Paper: The Climate for Private Investment in Brazil," March 27, 1962, Box 112, Goulart Visit, POF, JFK.

24. Gordon interview, January 19, 1976.

25. Ibid.

26. Ibid.

27. See Skidmore, *Politics in Brazil*, pp. 191, 200–201.

28. Lincoln Gordon, "Points Supplementary to R. N. Goodwin Draft of 1–1–62 [*sic*]," January 7, 1962, Box 12 and 13, Brazil Vol. 2, NSF, JFK.

29. Attachment to memorandum from Richard Goodwin to McGeorge Bundy, February 7, 1962, Box 12 and 13, Brazil Vol. 2, NSF, JFK.

30. Ibid.

31. Lincoln Gordon, "Points Supplementary to R. N. Goodwin Draft of 1–1–62."

32. Dulles, *Unrest in Brazil*, p. 169.

33. Campos interview, p. 41.

34. Ibid., p. 40.

35. Herbert K. May, treasury attaché, U.S. Embassy, Rio to State Department, January 23, 1961, Box 112, Brazil, Security, 1961, POF, JFK.

36. Skidmore, *Politics in Brazil*, pp. 191, 194–195.

37. Ibid., pp. 194, 196–197.

38. "Position Paper: Additional Financial Assistance to Goulart," April 3, 1962, Box 112, Goulart Visit, POF, JFK.

39. Ibid.

40. Dulles, *Unrest in Brazil*, pp. 161–167.

41. Gordon interview, January 19, 1976.

42. "Intelligence Memorandum: Raul Francisco Ryff," March 30, 1962, Box 112-A, CFB, Security, 1962, POF, JFK.

43. Campos interview, p. 24.

44. Geneen to Kennedy, February 17, 1962, Box 12 and 13, Brazil Vol. 2, NSF, JFK.

45. Gordon to Rusk, February 25, 1962, Box 12, POF, JFK.

46. Rusk to Gordon, March 7, 1962, Box 12, POF, JFK.

47. Rusk to U.S. Embassy, Rio de Janeiro, March 3, 1962, Box 12, POF, JFK.

48. Ibid.

49. "Position Paper: Additional Financial Assistance for Brazil," March 3, 1962, Box 112, Goulart Visit, POF, JFK.

50. Gordon interview, January 19, 1976.

51. *U.S. Code Annotated*, Title 22: 2370.

52. L. D. Battle to McGeorge Bundy, "Scope Paper," March 26, 1962, Box 112, Goulart Visit, POF, JFK.

53. Ibid.

54. Gordon to Rusk, March 14, 1962, Box 12, POF, JFK.

55. Campos interview, p. 24.

56. Ibid., pp. 25–26.

57. Gordon to Rusk, March 15, 1962, Box 12 and 13, POF, JFK.

58. Campos interview, pp. 26–27.

59. Ibid., pp. 26–28; "Position Paper: Brazil's Desire for a Sugar Quota," March 26, 1962, Box 112, Goulart Visit, POF, JFK; "Position Paper: Coffee Stabilization Agreement," March 26, 1962, Box 112, Goulart Visit, POF, JFK. The presidents also discussed sugar quotas, with Goulart pushing for such a quota and Kennedy suggesting the advantages of abolishing all sugar quotas. Goulart urged active U.S. support of an international coffee agreement that the United States stood ready to negotiate even though it was concerned about the overproduction of coffee in Brazil.

60. Campos interview, pp. 27–28.

61. Ibid., pp. 28–29.

62. Ibid., p. 29.

63. Ibid., pp. 30–31.

64. Gordon interview, January 19, 1976.

65. Campos interview, p. 34.

66. Skidmore, *Politics in Brazil*, p. 218.

67. Gordon interview, January 19, 1976.

68. "CIA Information Report," May 29, 1962, Box 12 and 13, Brazil, POF, JFK.

69. Gordon to Rusk, June 5, 1962, Box 112-A, CFB, Security, 1962, POF, JFK.

70. Ibid.

71. Ibid.

72. "Position Paper: Development of Brazilian Shale-Oil Industry," March 29, 1962, Box 112, Goulart Visit, POF, JFK.

73. Gordon to Rusk, June 5, 1962, Box 112-A, CFB, Security, 1962, POF, JFK.

74. Ibid.

75. Dulles, *Unrest in Brazil*, p. 170.

76. Attachment to letter from William H. Brubeck to McGeorge Bundy, July 28, 1962, Box 112-A, CFB, Security, 1962, POF, JFK.

77. Dulles, *Unrest in Brazil*, pp. 171–172.

78. Gordon interview, January 19, 1976.

79. Dulles, *Unrest in Brazil*, p. 173.

80. Gordon interview, January 19, 1976; Dulles, *Unrest in Brazil*, p. 174.

81. Gordon interview, January 19, 1976.

82. Dulles, *Unrest in Brazil*, pp. 178–179.

83. JFK to Fowler Hamilton, February 5, 1962, Box 112, Brazil, Security, POF, JFK. A CIA intelligence report sent to President Kennedy in early April also emphasized the importance of the October elections. The report noted "a significant growth in leftist and nationalist sentiment in Brazil. These elements will probably substantially increase their present strength in Congress" (attachment to correspondence from John McCone to JFK, April 2, 1962, JFK).

84. Riordan Roett, *The Politics of Foreign Aid*, p. 173.

85. Gordon interview, January 19, 1976. The first loan agreement for COPERBO was signed in September 1962 for $3.4 million. A second loan agreement for $3.3 million was signed

in August 1963 (Roett, *Politics of Foreign Aid*, p. 140). Attempts to make COPERBO profitable were unsuccessful, and
finally the lending institutions involved tried quietly to dis-
associate themselves from the project.

86. Roberto Garcia, "Castello perdeu a batalha" [trans.
David Parker], *Veja*, March 9, 1977, p. 6.

87. Vernon Walters interview, January 20, 1976; Gordon
interview, January 19, 1976.

88. Gordon interview, January 19, 1976.

89. Ibid.

90. Ibid.; Walters interview.

91. Campos interview, p. 40.

92. Gordon interview, January 19, 1976.

93. Ibid.

94. Dulles, *Unrest in Brazil*, p. 194.

95. Campos interview, p. 44.

96. Ibid., pp. 44–45.

97. Ibid., p. 45; Gordon interview, January 19, 1976; *Jornal
do Brasil* quoted in Dulles, *Unrest in Brazil*, p. 195.

98. Campos interview, p. 45.

99. Roett, *Politics of Foreign Aid*, p. 90.

100. Skidmore, *Politics in Brazil*, p. 218.

101. Ibid., p. 403 n. 57.

102. Dulles, *Unrest in Brazil*, p. 236.

103. Furtado estimated that in 1962 debt repayments and
profit remittances reached $564 million, 45 percent of the value
of Brazil's exports during that same period (see Skidmore,
Politics in Brazil, p. 238).

104. Ibid., p. 238; Dulles, *Unrest in Brazil*, pp. 200–201.

105. Lincoln Gordon interview with John E. Reilly, p. 61.

106. Gordon interview, January 19, 1976.

107. Quoted in Attachment to Memorandum to JFK from
Ralph Dungan, February 1, 1963, Box 62, Staff Memorandum,
Dungan, POF, JFK.

108. David Bell to Kennedy, March 4, 1963, Box 12, POF,
JFK.

109. Campos interview, p. 46.

110. Gordon interview, JFK, p. 60.

111. Ibid., p. 62.

112. Ibid.

113. Goulart to Kennedy, March 8, 1963, Box 112, Brazil, Security, POF, JFK.

114. Ibid.

115. Campos interview, p. 47.

116. Bell to San Tiago Dantas, March 25, 1963, Box 112-A, CFB, Security, 1963, POF, JFK.

117. Dantas to Bell, March 25, 1963, attachment to correspondence from William H. Brubeck to McGeorge Bundy, March 24, 1963, Box 112-A, CFB, Security, 1963, POF, JFK.

118. Campos interview, p. 48.

119. Gordon interview, JFK, p. 63.

120. "Current Intelligence Memorandum: Plotting against Goulart," March 8, 1963, Box 112-A, CFB, Security, 1963, POF, JFK.

121. Skidmore, *Politics in Brazil*, p. 239.

122. Dantas to Bell, March 25, 1963, Box 112-A, CFB, Security, 1963, POF, JFK.

123. Skidmore, *Politics in Brazil*, pp. 242–243.

124. Campos interview, p. 49.

125. Gordon to Rusk, April 9, 1963, Box 112-A, CFB, Security, 1963, POF, JFK.

126. Ibid.

127. Ibid.

128. Ibid.; Gordon interview, January 19, 1976.

129. Skidmore, *Politics in Brazil*, p. 245.

130. Campos interview, p. 50.

131. William Brubeck to McGeorge Bundy, May 7, 1963, Box 112-A, CFB, Security, 1963, POF, JFK.

132. U.S. Senate, *Nomination of Lincoln Gordon*, p. 34.

133. Dulles, *Unrest in Brazil*, pp. 176, 210.

134. Gordon interview, JFK, p. 65.

135. Dulles, *Unrest in Brazil*, p. 214.

136. Gordon to Rusk, July 17, 1963, and Rusk to U.S. Embassy, Rio de Janeiro, July 26, 1963, Box 13 and 14, Brazil Vol. 6, NSF, JFK.

137. See Braddock to Rusk, May 8, 1963; Braddock to Rusk,

May 10, 1963; and Feldman to Department of State, August 16, 1963, Box 13 and 14, Brazil Vol. 6, NSF, JFK.

138. Braddock to Department of State, August 16, 1963, Box 13 and 14, Brazil Vol. 6, NSF, JFK.

139. Ibid.

140. Constitution of the United States of Brazil, 1946, Title VII, Article 177.

141. Raymond Estep, *The Military in Brazilian Politics, 1821–1970*, p. 92.

142. Vernon Walters, Department of Defense Intelligence Information Report, August 6, 1963, Box 2, Schlesinger File, JFK. This report gives the names of "ultranationalists" who were promoted or given better assignments and of "pro-US officers" who were often passed over or retired by Goulart.

143. Estep, *Military in Brazilian Politics*, pp. 100–101.

144. Dungan to Kennedy and Attachment, September 27, 1963, Box 62, Staff Memorandum, Dungan, POF, JFK.

145. Joint Department of State–AID Message to U.S. Embassy Rio de Janeiro, September 24, 1963, Box 12 and 13, Brazil Vol. 7, NSF, JFK.

146. Gordon interview, January 19, 1976. The files of Arthur Schlesinger, assistant to the president, contained an article by Holmes Alexander entitled "A Cuba—or a China?" from the October 24, 1963, issue of the *Maryland Monitor*. The article was sent to Schlesinger by John Plank at the State Department. The article criticized Gordon's "islands of sanity" policy as too liberal and suggested that "a time soon may come to ask ourselves whether it is in our self-interest to have Goulart stagger on till the end of his term in 1965—or whether our interests would be better served if Goulart were 'retired' ahead of schedule . . . the only alternative to expect would be a communist-type takeover" (attachment to correspondence from Plank to Schlesinger, October 29, 1963, Box 2, Schlesinger File, JFK).

147. Gordon interview, January 19, 1976.

148. Ibid.

149. Niles Bond, minister consul general, São Paulo, to the State Department, January 16, 1963, CFB Vol. 1, NSF, JFK.

150. The Brazilian Constitution of 1946 gave the Congress

the power to declare a state of siege during war or during "serious domestic disturbance or facts evidencing its imminent outbreak" (Constitution of the United States of Brazil, 1946, Title IX, Art. 206).

151. Skidmore, *Politics in Brazil*, p. 263; Dulles, *Unrest in Brazil*, pp. 236–237.

152. Gordon interview, January 19, 1976; Dulles, *Unrest in Brazil*, p. 246.

153. Skidmore, *Politics in Brazil*, pp. 265–266.

154. Gordon interview, JFK, p. 66.

155. Campos interview, p. 52.

156. Quoted in Gordon to Rusk, November 20, 1963, Box 13 and 14, Brazil Vol. 7, NSF, JFK. This document notes that the "interview" was actually drafted by members of Goulart's staff and had been submitted to the magazine five days earlier.

157. Ibid.

158. Ibid.

159. Skidmore, *Politics in Brazil*, p. 268.

160. Gordon to Rusk, November 20, 1963, Box 13 and 14, Brazil Vol. 7, NSF, JFK.

161. Gordon interview, JFK, pp. 67–69.

162. Campos interview, p. 53.

163. Gordon interview, JFK, pp. 55 and 68.

164. Goulart to Johnson, December 13, 1963, Presidential Correspondence—Brazil, LBJ.

165. Philip Geyelin, *Lyndon B. Johnson and the World*, p. 97.

166. Robert A. Packenham, *Liberal America and the Third World*, p. 94.

167. Thomas Mann interview, November 20, 1975, Austin, Texas. Mann was a former ambassador to Mexico who had served in positions of high responsibility with the State Department under three previous presidents.

168. Gordon Chase to McGeorge Bundy, November 27, 1963, CFB Vol. 1, NSF, LBJ.

169. Gordon to Rusk, April 9, 1963, Box 112-A, CFB, Security, 1963, POF, JFK.

170. David Rockefeller to Johnson, November 29, 1963,

Name File, Business D–G, WHCF, LBJ.

171. Johnson to Rockefeller, December 11, 1963, Name File, Business D–G, WHCF, LBJ.

172. Skidmore, *Politics in Brazil*, pp. 266–268.

173. Gordon interview, January 19, 1976.

174. Ibid.

175. Ibid.

176. Ibid.

177. Ibid.; Skidmore, *Politics in Brazil*, pp. 227, 271.

178. Gordon interview, January 19, 1976.

179. Quoted in Gordon to Rusk, January 18, 1964, CFB Vol. 1, NSF, LBJ.

180. Rusk to U.S. Embassy, Rio de Janeiro, February 18, 1964, CFB Vol. 1, NSF, LBJ.

181. Gordon to Rusk, February 18, 1964, CFB Vol. 1, NSF, LBJ.

182. Campos interview, p. 56.

183. Gordon interview, January 19, 1976.

184. Estep, *Military in Brazilian Politics*, p. 115.

185. Walters interview.

186. Ibid.

187. Gordon to Rusk, Attn: Thomas Mann, March 4, 1964, CFB Vol. 1, NSF, LBJ.

188. *Brazil Herald*, March 12, 1964, p. 1.

189. Ibid., March 14, 1964, p. 1.

190. Quoted in Dulles, *Unrest in Brazil*, p. 270 from *Correio da Manha*, March 14, 1964.

191. Skidmore, *Politics in Brazil*, p. 288; Dulles, *Unrest in Brazil*, p. 269.

192. In late 1963, Goulart told Gordon of a scheme he had whereby narrow strips of unused land on either side of federal highways would be expropriated for peasant use. Gordon told Goulart that the problem, as he understood it, had to do with large amounts of unused land and too many people in the Northeast section of Brazil and that it seemed whimsical to take strips of land along highways and call that land reform. Goulart responded, "Oh, I know all that, but this will get those PSD [conservative political party] colonels where it hurts." Gordon

viewed these land reform measures as politically motivated to serve Goulart's personal ambitions (Gordon interview, January 19, 1976).

193. Quoted in Skidmore, *Politics in Brazil*, p. 288.

194. Dulles, *Unrest in Brazil*, p. 271, from *O Estado de São Paulo*, March 14, 1964.

195. Dulles, *Unrest in Brazil*, pp. 271–272.

196. Walters interview; see also Vernon Walters, *Silent Missions*, p. 383.

197. Gordon interview, January 19, 1978.

198. Dan Kurzman, "LBJ Seen Reaffirming Latin Aid Today," *Washington Post*, March 16, 1964, p. 9a.

199. Ibid.

200. Tad Szulc, "U.S. May Abandon Effort to Deter Latin Dictators," *New York Times*, March 19, 1964, p. 1.

201. Ibid.

202. Gordon interview, January 19, 1976.

203. Mann interview, February 10, 1976.

204. Gordon interview, January 19, 1976.

205. Ibid.

206. Walters interview.

207. According to *O Estado de São Paulo*, the resignation of Pierre Salinger, the press secretary of both Kennedy and Johnson, was used to mark a contrast in Kennedy's and Johnson's policies that thenceforth were to be guided "by national interest and by the circumstances in which the situation arose."

208. Dulles, *Unrest in Brazil*, p. 276.

209. Gordon interview, January 19, 1976.

210. Gordon interview, January 23, 1976.

211. A precedent for a presidential coup had been set by Getulio Vargas in his 1937 seizure of dictatorial power. The precedent had not been lost on Goulart. During the week after Gordon returned from Washington, he and former President Kubitschek had met and discussed the rapidly evolving events in Brazil. At that meeting, Kubitschek told the ambassador a story regarding Goulart while he was Kubitschek's vice-president. Goulart, noting Kubitschek's strong support, had said on more than one occasion: "Juscelino, I don't understand you; you are so popular, *da o golpe* [stage a coup—stay in office]. Some of the press will fuss a bit, but everyone will get over it." Gordon

believed that Goulart wanted a "superversion" or "overmining" of the system—an overthrow from above (Gordon interview, January 19, 1976).

212. Gordon to Rusk et al., teleconference, March 27, 1964, CFB Vol. 2, NSF, LBJ.

213. Lincoln Gordon, "Recollections of President Castelo Branco," p. 2.

214. Gordon to Rusk, Attn: T. Mann and White House, March 26, 1964, CFB Vol. 2, NSF, LBJ.

215. Walters interview.

216. Gordon to Rusk et al., teleconference, March 27, 1964, CFB Vol. 2, NSF, LBJ.

217. Ibid.

218. Ibid.

219. Ibid.

220. Ibid.

221. Gordon interview, January 19, 1976; Walters interview.

222. Walters interview.

223. Antonieta Diniz and Paulo Castelo Branco interview with John W. F. Dulles, Rio de Janeiro, December 13, 1975.

224. Gordon interview, January 19, 1976.

225. Alberto Byington, a Brazilian educated in the United States, had contacted embassy personnel for a U.S. commitment to provide contingent support in the anti-Goulart conspiracy. He had suggested the potential threat posed by Goulart's Petrobrás support. Byington privately bought two shiploads of oil and had it stored as alternate backing for a military coup (Walters interview).

226. Gordon interview, January 19, 1976; Walters interview.

227. Ibid.

228. Gordon to Rusk et al., teleconference, March 27, 1964, CFB Vol. 2, NSF, LBJ.

229. Ibid.

230. Gordon interviews, January 19 and 23, 1976.

231. Estep, *Military in Brazilian Politics*, pp. 111–112; Dulles, *Unrest in Brazil*, pp. 279–285; Skidmore, *Politics in Brazil*, pp. 296–298.

232. Dulles, *Unrest in Brazil*, pp. 288–289; Skidmore, *Politics in Brazil*, p. 265.

233. Dulles, *Unrest in Brazil*, pp. 290–293; Estep,

Military in Brazilian Politics, p. 113.

234. Quoted in Gordon to Rusk, March 31, 1964, CFB Vol. 2, NSF, LBJ.

235. Dulles, *Unrest in Brazil*, pp. 313–314.

236. Skidmore, *Politics in Brazil*, p. 300.

237. Gordon interview, January 19, 1976.

238. Rusk to U.S. Embassy, Rio de Janeiro, March 30, 1964, CFB Vol. 2, NSF, LBJ.

239. Rusk to U.S. Embassy, Brasilia et al., March 30, 1964, CFB Vol. 2, NSF, LBJ. Following normal procedures, U.S. consulates would have directed their messages to the Rio de Janeiro embassy, which would have in turn relayed them to Washington.

240. Walters describes his possession of this preliminary knowledge as the result of a process of elimination. The Brazilians would not plan a revolution on a holiday, such as Easter, Palm Sunday, Good Friday, or even April Fool's Day. He also believed the conspirators thought there was some urgency to making a coup before Goulart himself made a presidential coup and before Goulart further damaged military discipline or promoted men loyal to himself over those with more traditional loyalties (Walters interview).

241. Bond to Rusk, March 30, 1964, CFB Vol. 2, NSF, LBJ.

242. Rusk to Gordon, March 30, 1964, CFB Vol. 2, NSF, LBJ.

243. Gordon via Rusk for Bundy, McNamara, and McCone, March 31, 1964, CFB Vol. 2, NSF, LBJ.

244. "Agenda for meeting on Brazil," CFB Vol. 2, NSF, LBJ; and Message for U.S. Embassy, Rio de Janeiro, March 31, 1964, CFB Vol. 2, NSF, LBJ.

245. Declassified cables suggest that arms and ammunition plans for Brazil were developed under the U.S. commander in chief of southern forces in Panama in 1961 (called USCINCSO Contingency Plan 2–61). Such plans are developed to respond to possible crises, are maintained at the Pentagon, and are generally reviewed annually (see JCS to CSAF et al. 010102Z April 1964, CFB Vol. 3, NSF, LBJ). The cables I have seen do not indicate who approved action on this plan on March 31, 1964, although cables describing this operation were sent by

Joint Chiefs of Staff. I assume that the decision to activate such plans would begin at the Pentagon and would eventually include officials at the State Department, the White House, and the CIA.

246. Message for U.S. Embassy, Rio de Janeiro, March 31, 1964, CFB Vol. 2, NSF, LBJ.

247. While these governors were not named, I would assume the group would include those mentioned in other cables as "crystallizing overt support for the constitution . . . and for rejection of communism . . . Lacerda of Guanabara, Adhemar de Barros of São Paulo, Menghetti of Rio Grande do Sul, Braga of Paraná, and . . . Magalhaes Pinto of Minas Gerais" (see Gordon to Rusk et al., teleconference, March 27, 1964, CFB Vol. 2, NSF, LBJ).

248. Ibid.

249. Ibid.

250. Gordon to Rusk, March 31, 1964, CFB Vol. 2, NSF, LBJ.

251. Message for U.S. Embassy, Rio de Janeiro, March 31, 1964, CFB Vol. 2, NSF, LBJ.

252. JCS to CINCLANT, 311907Z March 1964, CFB Vol. 2, NSF, LBJ.

253. CINCLANTFLT to COMSECONDFLT, 312250Z March 1964, CFB Vol. 3, NSF, LBJ.

254. CSAF to ZEN/MATS et al., 011644Z April 1964, CFB Vol. 3, NSF, LBJ.

255. JCS to USCINCSO, 010101Z April 1964, CFB Vol. 3, NSF, LBJ.

256. JCS to CSAF et al., 010102Z April 1964, CFB Vol. 3, NSF, LBJ.

257. Ibid.

258. The tankers, under contract to Military Sea Transport Services, included the *Santa Inez*, the *Chepachet*, the *Hampton Roads*, and the *Nash Bulk* (JCS to DSA et al., 010103Z April 1964, CFB Vol. 3, NSF, LBJ).

259. Quoted in Gordon to Rusk, March 31, 1964, CFB Vol. 2, NSF, LBJ.

260. Gordon teleconference, no date, no named recipients [judging from the contents, I think the message was written

by Lincoln Gordon in response to Ball, Mann, and Dungan in Washington, March 31, 1964], CFB Vol. 2, (Item 61), NSF, LBJ.

261. Ibid.

262. Gordon et al. [to Ball et al.] teleconference, attachment to Ball et al. (to Gordon, et al.), 1500Z, April 1, 1964 [some teleconferences are recorded in Z time without writing out the full date-time group], CFB Vol. 2 (Item 59), NSF, LBJ; Gordon interview, January 19, 1976.

263. Brayner had been informing Walters of expected movements in the conspiracy (see JANAF Attachés Brazil, Action White House, J-5 et al., 311800Z March 1964, CFB Vol. 3, NSF, LBJ).

264. Brayner interview with John W. F. Dulles, Rio de Janeiro, October 6, 1975.

265. USCINCSO to COMUSARSO et al., 011900Z April 1964, CFB Vol. 3, NSF, LBJ.

266. Capt. Thomas V. Solan interview, March 10, 1976, Austin, Texas.

267. Joint Message J-9 for AFCIN, ACSI, and DNI, no date [apparently written in the early afternoon of April 1], CFB Vol. 3 (Item 34), NSF, LBJ.

268. Ball [to Gordon et al.], teleconference, 1500Z, April 1, 1964, CFB Vol. 2 (Item 59), NSF, LBJ.

269. Gordon et al. [to Ball et al.], teleconference, 1500Z, April 1, 1964, and Ball et al. [to Gordon et al.], teleconference, 1500Z, April 1, 1964, CFB Vol. 2 (Item 59), NSF, LBJ.

270. Gordon to Rusk, April 1, 1964, CFB Vol. 3, NSF, LBJ.

271. Gordon interview, January 19, 1976.

272. Joint Message J-9 for AFCIN, ACSI, and DNI, no date [probably written in the early afternoon of April 1], CFB Vol. 3 (Item 34), NSF, LBJ; Gordon et al. [to Ball et al.], teleconference, 021500Z, CFB Vol. 2 (Item 57), NSF, LBJ. See also Gordon to Rusk, April 2, 1964, CFB Vol. 3 (Item 105), NSF, LBJ. In his memoirs, Walters has played down the political importance of his contacts with Castelo Branco (see *Silent Missions*, pp. 383, 391); at the time, however, given the cables and other messages being sent from the Rio embassy to Washington, there was some significance attached to these meetings.

273. A CIA Biographic Intelligence Bulletin described Maz-zilli as a "cautious practitioner of the possible," and a "middle-of-the-roader." The biography noted that Mazzilli had "amassed considerable wealth, but [that] his riches were not inherited; rather, they were accumulated during an arduous climb to the top of the bureaucratic heap" ("Paschoal Ranieri Mazzilli: In-terim President of Brazil," CIA Biographic Intelligence Bulle-tin, April 2, 1964, CFB, NSF, LBJ).

274. Gordon to Rusk, April 1, 1964, CFB Vol. 3, NSF, LBJ.

275. Gordon interviews, January 19 and 23, 1976.

276. Joint Message, J-9 for AFCIN, ACSI, and DNI, no date [probably written in the early afternoon of April 1], CFB Vol. 3 (Item 34), NSF, LBJ.

277. Gordon interview, January 19, 1976.

278. Gordon et al. [to Ball et al.], teleconference, 2030Z, April 1, 1964, CFB Vol. 2 (Item 58), NSF, LBJ.

279. Ball et al. [to Gordon et al.], teleconference, 2030Z, April 1, 1964, CFB Vol. 2 (Item 58), NSF, LBJ.

280. Embassy cables from this period refer to the military conspirators as the "democrats" or the "democratic forces."

281. Gordon to Rusk, April 2, 1964, CFB Vol. 3 (Item 103), NSF, LBJ.

282. Gordon et al. [to Ball et al.], teleconference, 021900Z, April 1964, CFB Vol. 2 (Item 56), NSF, LBJ.

283. Gordon to Rusk, April 2, 1964, CFB Vol. 3, NSF, LBJ.

284. Ball et al. [to Gordon et al.], teleconference, 1500Z, April 2, 1964, CFB Vol. 2 (Item 57), NSF, LBJ.

285. Mann to Gordon, April 2, 1964, CFB Vol. 3, NSF, LBJ.

286. Ibid.

287. Gordon to Rusk to White House, Attn: Mr. Bundy for Senator Carl Hayden, April 2, 1964, CFB Vol. 3, NSF, LBJ.

288. Gordon to Rusk, April 2, 1964, NSF, CFB Vol. 3 (Item 103), NSF, LBJ.

289. Gordon et al. [to Ball et al.], teleconference, 1500Z, April 2, 1964, CFB Vol. 2 (Item 57), NSF, LBJ.

290. Gordon interview, January 19, 1976.

291. Ball et al. [to Gordon et al.], teleconference, 2300Z, April 2, 1964, CFB Vol. 2 (Item 55), NSF, LBJ.

292. Gordon interview, January 19, 1976.

293. Gordon et al. [to Ball et al.], teleconference, 2300Z, April 2, 1964, CFB Vol. 2 (Item 55), NSF, LBJ.

294. Gordon interview, January 19, 1976.

295. Ball et al. [to Gordon et al.], teleconference, 2300Z, April 2, 1964, CFB Vol. 2 (Item 55), NSF, LBJ.

296. Gordon interview, January 19, 1976.

297. Gordon et al. [to Ball et al.], teleconference, 2300Z, April 2, 1964, and Ball et al. (to Gordon et al.) teleconference, 2300Z, April 2, 1964, CFB Vol. 2 (Item 55), NSF, LBJ.

298. Ibid.

299. Quoted in U.S. Department of State News Release, "Historical Chronology: U.S. Policy toward Governments of Brazil, 1821–Present," August 1973, p. 10.

300. Rusk to U.S. Embassy, Montevideo, Uruguay, April 2, 1964, CFB Vol. 3, NSF, LBJ.

301. CINCLANTFLT to COMSECONDFLT and COM-SERVLANT, 031750Z April 1964, CFB Vol. 3, NSF, LBJ.

302. This joint task force commanded by Maj. Gen. Breitweiser had already terminated operations at 5:00 P.M. Rio time on April 2, 1964. See USCINCSO to COMUSARSO 021722Z April 1964, CFB Vol. 3, NSF, LBJ.

303. USCINCSO to JCS 031724Z April 1964, CFB Vol. 3, NSF, LBJ.

304. Gordon interview, January 19, 1976.

305. JCS to CSA et al. 032214Z April 1964, CFB Vol. 3, NSF, LBJ.

306. JCS to CSA et al. 072309Z April 1964, CFB Vol. 3, NSF, LBJ.

307. Now there is also a third type of loan called a "sector loan." Sector loans are granted for a broad category of assistance, such as education or health.

308. The ambassador's relationship with the ministers of finance varied, but one indication of rapport between Gordon and at least one minister was the fact that Carvalho Pinto asked the ambassador to speak for him at loan negotiations in Washington after the Brazilian Minister had to return to Brazil unexpectedly in response to Goulart's request that Congress declare a state of siege (Gordon interview, January 19, 1976).

309. Quoted and translated in Octavio Ianni, *Crisis in Brazil*, trans. Phyllis R. Evelyth, p. 146.

310. Mann interviews, November 12 and 24, 1975.

311. See earlier reference, p. 82.

312. Gordon interview, January 19, 1976.

313. Lincoln Gordon has described the Bell-Dantas Agreement as "foreshadowing a program loan" status.

314. U.S. Senate, Committee on Foreign Relations, Subcommittee on Western Hemisphere Affairs, *United States Policies and Programs in Brazil*, May 4, 5, and 11, 1971, p. 186.

315. Ibid.

316. Ibid., pp. 189–191. Loans to private enterprises and to enterprises that had a mixture of private and governmental ownership tended to concentrate in, but were not limited to, the same years. The remainder of the loans were negotiated with the federal government or federally owned enterprises.

317. Kennedy to Fowler Hamilton, February 5, 1962, Box 112, Brazil, Security, POF, JFK.

318. Roett, *The Politics of Foreign Aid*, pp. 130–132; Gordon interview, January 19, 1976; Robert Ballantyne interview.

319. Roett, *The Politics of Foreign Aid*, pp. 141–169.

320. See *U.S. Policies and Programs in Brazil* for a description of the Public Safety Program's purpose, funding, and training. The program received criticism in the U.S. Congress because of stories in the press of repression and torture that people suffered at the hands of the Brazilian police, and the program was phased out in the early seventies.

321. See Agency for International Development, *U.S. Overseas Loans and Grants and Assistance from International Organizations*. This report was prepared for the use of those congressional committees primarily concerned with foreign aid and is a useful document for comparing assistance figures with those of other Latin American countries.

322. Gordon to Rusk, Attn: Mann, March 4, 1964, CFB Vol. 1, NSF, LBJ.

323. Gordon interview, January 19, 1976.

324. "Background Paper: Brazil," Attachment to Memorandum from L. P. Battle to Richard N. Goodwin, September 14,

1961, Box 112, Brazil, Security, 1961, POF, JFK.

325. Gordon to Rusk, Attn: Mann, March 4, 1964, CFB Vol. 1, NSF, LBJ.

326. The literature on repression and torture in Brazil is extensive. For example, see Rieck B. Hannifin's *Repression of Civil Liberties and Human Rights in Brazil since the Revolution of 1964*; Fred B. Morris, "In the Presence of Mine Enemies: Faith and Torture in Brazil," *Harper's Magazine*, October 1975, pp. 57–70; Ralph della Cava, "Torture in Brazil," *Commonweal*, April 24, 1970, pp. 135–141; Philippe C. Schmitter, "The Persecution of Political and Social Scientists in Brazil," *P.S.: Political Science* 3 (1970): 123–128; and U.S. Senate, *The Congressional Record*, May 10, 1976, S6754–S6758.

327. Edmar Morel, *O Golpe Começou em Washington*.

328. Gordon to Ralph Dungan, April 13, 1964, Name File—Lincoln Gordon, WHCF, LBJ.

329. U.S. Senate, *Nomination of Lincoln Gordon*, p. 44.

LIST OF SOURCES

Unpublished

Ballantyne, Robert. Interview with the author. Washington, D.C., January 21, 1976.

Burlando, Everett J. Interview with the author. Washington, D.C., January 22, 1976.

Brayner, Floriano de Lima II. Interview with John W. F. Dulles. Rio de Janeiro, November 25, 1975.

"Brazil's Balance of Payments, 1955–1969, Table." American Embassy Rio de Janeiro. State Department files, Washington, D.C.

Campos, Roberto de Oliveira. Interview with John E. Reilly. Rio de Janeiro, May 29 and 30, 1964. Oral History. John F. Kennedy Presidential Library, Waltham, Massachusetts.

Diniz, Antonieta, and Castelo Branco, Paulo. Interview with John W. F. Dulles. Rio de Janeiro, December 13, 1975.

Gordon, Lincoln. Interviews with the author. Washington, D.C., January 19 and 23, 1976.

———. Interview with John E. Reilly. Rio de Janeiro, May 30, 1964. Oral History. John F. Kennedy Presidential Library, Waltham, Massachusetts.

———. "Recollections of President Castelo Branco." Manuscript in author's possession.

"How Much Aid Money in Total Has Been Spent in the Northeast?" State Department Files, Washington, D.C. [copy in author's possession].

Mann, Thomas C. Interviews with the author. Austin, Texas, November 12 and 24, 1975; telephone interview, February 10, 1976.

National Security Files. Agency Files. Lyndon Baines Johnson Presidential Library, Austin, Texas.

————. Brazil, Vols. 1–7. John F. Kennedy Presidential Library, Waltham, Massachusetts.

————. Country Files: Brazil, Vols. 1–6. Lyndon Baines Johnson Presidential Library, Austin, Texas.

Presidential Office Files. Country Files: Brazil: Goulart Visit. John F. Kennedy Presidential Library, Waltham, Massachusetts.

————. Country Files: Brazil, 1960–1963. John F. Kennedy Presidential Library, Waltham, Massachusetts.

————. Country Files: Brazil, Security, 1961–1963. John F. Kennedy Presidential Library, Waltham, Massachusetts.

————. Staff Memoranda, Boxes 62, 65, and 66. John F. Kennedy Presidential Library, Waltham, Massachusetts.

Schlesinger, Arthur, Jr. Personal Papers, Brazil. John F. Kennedy Presidential Library, Waltham, Massachusetts.

Solan, Thomas V. (Captain, U.S. Navy). Interview with the author. Austin, Texas, March 10, 1976.

Special Files. Head of State Files: Branco Correspondence, Brazil. Lyndon Baines Johnson Presidential Library, Austin, Texas.

————. Presidential Correspondence, Brazil. Lyndon Baines Johnson Presidential Library, Austin, Texas.

U.S. Agency for International Development, Brazil, Comptrollers Office. "USAID/Brazil: Financial Status of AID Administered Country Loans as of April 30, 1965, and as of May 31, 1965." State Department Files, Washington, D.C.

"United States Assistance to Brazil: Summary as of June 30, 1972." State Department Files, Washington, D.C.

Walters, Vernon A. "Humberto de Alencar Castelo Branco." Manuscript in author's possession.

————. Interview with the author. McLean, Virginia, January 20, 1976.

White House Name Files. Business Group for Latin America. Lyndon Baines Johnson Presidential Library, Austin, Texas.

————. Lincoln Gordon, Lyndon Baines Johnson Presidential Library, Austin, Texas.

————. Thomas Mann. Lyndon Baines Johnson Presidential Library, Austin, Texas.

Published

Bandeira, Moniz. *O Governo João Goulart: As Lutas Sociais no Brasil*. Rio de Janeiro: Editôra Civilização Brasileira, 1977.

———. *Presença dos Estados Unidos no Brasil: Dois seculos de historia*. Rio de Janeiro: Editôra Civilização Brasileira, 1973.

Brasil, Presidencia da República. *Plano Trienial de Desenvolvimento Economico e Social, 1963–1965*. Departamento de Imprensa Nacional, 1963.

Brazil Herald (Rio de Janeiro), March and April 1964.

Cabral, Castilho. *Tempos de Jânio, e outros tempos*. Rio de Janeiro: Editôra Civilização Brasileira, 1962.

Constitution of the United States of Brazil, 1946. Washington, D.C.: Pan American Union, 1958.

Correa, Marcos Sá. *1964 Visto e Comentado Pela Casa Branca*. Porto Alegre, Brazil: L & PM Editôres, 1977.

Dantas, San Tiago. *Politica Externa Independente*. Rio de Janeiro: Editôra Civilização Brasileira, 1962.

Della Cava, Ralph. "Torture in Brazil." *Commonweal*, April 24, 1970, pp. 135–141.

Dulles, John W. F. *Castello Branco: The Making of a Brazilian President*. Introduction by Roberto Campos. College Station: Texas A&M University Press, 1978.

———. *Unrest in Brazil: Political-Military Crisis, 1955–1964*. Austin: University of Texas Press, 1970.

Einaudi, Luigi R.; Maullin, Richard L.; and Stepan, Alfred C. *Latin American Security Issues*. Santa Monica, Calif.: RAND Corp., April 1969.

Einaudi, Luigi R., and Stepan, Alfred C. *Latin American Institutional Development: Changing Military Perspectives in Peru and Brazil*. RAND Corp., April 1971.

Estep, Raymond. *The Military in Brazilian Politics, 1821–1970*. Maxwell Air Force Base, Ala.: Air University, Aerospace Studies Institute, Documentary Research Division, 1971.

Fagen, Richard R., and Cornelius, Wayne A., Jr., eds. *Politi-*

cal Power in Latin America: Seven Confrontations. Engle-
wood Cliffs, N.J.: Prentice-Hall, 1970.

Garcia, Roberto. "Castello perdeu a batalha." *Veja*, March 9,
1977, pp. 3–8.

Geyelin, Philip. *Lyndon B. Johnson and the World*. New York:
Frederick A. Praeger, 1966.

Gordon, Lincoln. *A New Deal for Latin America*. Cambridge,
Mass.: Harvard University Press, 1963.

————. "The United States and Brazil: Partners in Progress."
Department of State Bulletin 54 (1966): 620–624.

Hannifin, Rieck B. *Repression of Civil Liberties and Human
Rights in Brazil Since the Revolution of 1964*. Washington,
D.C.: Library of Congress Legislative Reference Service,
June 26, 1970.

Horowitz, Irving Louis. *Revolution in Brazil: Politics and
Society in a Developing Nation*. New York: E. P. Dutton
& Co, 1964.

Ianni, Octavio. *Crisis in Brazil*. Trans. Phyllis R. Evelyth.
New York: Columbia University Press, 1970.

Kurzman, Dan. "LBJ Seen Reaffirming Latin Aid Today."
Washington Post, March 16, 1964, p. 9a.

Levinson, Jerome, and de Onis, Juan. *The Alliance That Lost
Its Way*. Chicago: Quadrangle Books, 1970.

Morel, Edmar. *O Golpe Começou em Washington*. Rio de
Janeiro: Editôra Civilização Brasileira, 1965.

Morison, Elting E. *The American Style*. New York: Harper
and Brothers, 1958.

Morris, Fred B. "In the Presence of Mine Enemies: Faith and
Torture in Brazil." *Harper's Magazine*, October 1975, pp.
57–70.

New York Times, 1963 and 1964.

O Estado de São Paulo, March and April 1964.

Packenham, Robert A. *Liberal America and the Third World*.
Princeton: Princeton University Press, 1973.

Roett, Riordan. *The Politics of Foreign Aid: In the Brazilian
Northeast*. Nashville: Vanderbilt University Press, 1962.

————, ed. *Brazil in the Sixties*. Nashville: Vanderbilt University Press, 1972.

Rowe, James W. "Revolution or Counterrevolution in Brazil? Part I: The Diverse Background." *American University Field Staff Reports*. East Coast South America Series 11 (No. 4), 1964.

—————. "Revolution or Counterrevolution in Brazil? Part II: From 'Black Friday' to the New Reforms." *American University Field Staff Reports*. East Coast South American Series II (No. 5), 1964.

Schmitter, Phillippe C. "The Persecution of Political and Social Scientists in Brazil." *P.S.: Political Science* 3 (1970): 123–228.

Schneider, Ronald M. *The Political System of Brazil: Emergence of a "Modernizing" Authoritarian Regime, 1964–1970*. New York: Columbia University Press, 1971.

Skidmore, Thomas E. *Politics in Brazil, 1930–1964: An Experiment in Democracy*. New York: Oxford University Press, 1967.

Stepan, Alfred. *The Military in Politics: Changing Patterns in Brazil*. Princeton: Princeton University Press, 1971.

U.S. Agency for International Development. *The Foreign Assistance Program* (annual reports to the Congress for fiscal years 1962, 1963, 1964, 1965). Washington, D.C.: Government Printing Office, various dates.

—————, Office of Financial Management, Statistics and Reports Division. "U.S. Overseas Loans and Grants and Assistance from International Organizations: Obligations and Loan Authorizations July 1, 1945–June 30, 1974." [Washington, D.C., 1974].

U.S. Department of State. *American Foreign Policy Current Documents 1961*. Washington, D.C.: Government Printing Office, 1965.

—————, Bureau of Public Affairs, Historical Office. "Historical Study: U.S. Policy Toward Latin America: Recognition and Non-Recognition of Governments and Interruptions in Diplomatic Relations, 1933–1974." Department of State Publication 8819, Interamerican Series, 109. Washington, D.C.: Department of State, June 1975.

—————, Historical Studies Division. "Historical Chronology:

U.S. Policy Toward Governments of Brazil, 1821–Present."
News Release, Office of Media Services, Bureau of Public
Affairs, August 1973.

U.S. General Accounting Office. *Report to the Congress: The
Brazilian Economic Boom: How Should We Relate to It?*
Washington, D.C.: Government Printing Office, 1974.

U.S. Senate. *The Congressional Record*, May 10, 1976.

————, Committee on Foreign Relations. *Nomination of Lincoln Gordon of Massachusetts to be Assistant Secretary of
State for Interamerican Affairs*. Washington, D.C.: Government Printing Office, February 7, 1966.

————, Subcommittee on Western Hemisphere Affairs. *United
States Policies and Programs in Brazil*. Washington, D.C.:
Government Printing Office, May 4, 5, and 11, 1971.

Walters, Vernon A. *Silent Missions*. Garden City, N.Y.:
Doubleday and Company, 1978.

INDEX